MW01147039

Shattered Reflections

Shattered Reflections

A Female Soldier's Unveiled Truth

Dallas R. Knight

T-
thanks for
the support!
learn & grow
Dallas

Deeds Publishing | Athens

Published by Deeds Publishing in Athens, GA
www.deedspublishing.com

Printed in The United States of America

Cover and interior design by Deeds Publishing

ISBN 978-

Books are available in quantity for promotional or premium use.
For information, email info@deedspublishing.com.

First Edition, 2023

10 9 8 7 6 5 4 3 2 1

This book is dedicated to Dana Johnson, my best friend. If it weren't for you, I wouldn't have had a journal to record my thoughts in. Thank you for the gift, friend.

CONTENTS

PREFACE

A Woman's Perspective of OIF 2003

I've read so many books about war time. Everything from heroic events to leadership driven methodologies. I can't think of one that was written from the perspective of a woman combat veteran. I have found books written by female combat veterans discussing talking points other than their time spent in combat. As well as books written by females about women who served in combat. But why not directly from the female soldier's mouth? I, by no means, am speaking on behalf of any of my sisters in arms. However, I do hope to inspire them to speak up and speak out.

This journal is a documented recollection of my memories and perspectives. All names have been changed to protect the identities of my fellow veterans unless they specifically gave me permission to use their name (in which case I give you full permission to heckle them). There are redacted sections containing confidential information. I invite you to allow your imagination to fill in the blanks.

BEFORE THE JOURNAL

I was a lost 17-year-old that had barely graduated high school, only then realizing the advantages of good grades and families with stature. My mom suggested I go into the military. What a crazy idea, I'd thought. I mean, it made sense being that we come from a multi-generational combat veteran family. But me?! No. So I did what any other young woman would do while faced with a difficult and dangerous sounding decision: I called my dad. I thought there was no way he would support this absurd notion. I don't remember his exact words, but it went something like, "That sounds like a great idea." Perfect, the one time they're in agreement.

It was July 2001. My mom drove me to the Army recruiter's office where I met Sergeant T. I had chosen the Army to pursue because most of my cousins were in the Air Force and I've never been one to fall in line. Plus, if I was going to go into the military, I wanted to be stereotyped into one of the more badass branches. Perfectly logical sense.

In hindsight, I would have opted for the Air Force, air conditioning, and satellite phones. When I was asked what I wanted to do in the Army, I had no idea how to answer. Who knew there was a whole world within a world? My recruiter advised me to take my Armed Services Vocational Aptitude Battery (ASVAB) test and that would help guide me. (More hindsight there that I'll keep to myself. But know this, recruiters are the car salesmen of the military. Don't be afraid to hustle them back.)

I have no idea what the test truly directed me toward, but somewhere between my first and second meeting with Sgt. T, coupled with his wise discussions, I decided to become a military police (MP) officer. I also decided that this was going to be my straight shot ticket to becoming a Drug Enforcement Administration (DEA) agent.

College paid for, check! Degree, check! Real life experience, check! What I didn't realize is how *real life* the experience would end up being.

I was slotted for basic training in January 2002. Until then, I was training with the Nevada Readiness Center one weekend a month and I started my first semester of college. The morning of September 11th, 2003 I woke up to my radio alarm clock and the station talking about "the building" being on fire. I figured they were talking about the Stratosphere tower in Las Vegas that had already caught fire during construction a couple of times. I turned off the alarm and proceeded to get ready for class. I poured myself a bowl of cereal and turned on the TV. In that moment my entire life changed, and I immediately became a soldier in a war-driven military.

I only went through basic training once and have nothing to compare it to, but I will say, we were training for war. I often felt the responsibility to push for impeccable performance from our drill sergeants. Here's something that many don't realize—even those in the military think that all MPs are stereotypical patrol or street cops. Not the case. Definitely not in my case.

Ninety percent of my military career was spent conducting combat missions, including enemy prisoner of war (EPW) camps, convoy security, and corrections (jail) operations.

I don't remember exactly when the warning order came, never mind the official orders, but I know from records that our deployment started February 10, 2003. The beginning of our deployment was a few months of gruesome training at Fort Lewis, Washington. I debated on sharing any detail from during that time and decided against it. With that said, Ft. Lewis could be summarized with: lots of scenario trainings, lots of booze, and lots of money spent on ridiculous things. Although, I do share some brief insight in the first journal entry. Basically, we all lived like we were never coming back, because honestly, we didn't think we were.

THE JOURNAL

May 3, 2003

So here I am sitting in the hanger [Fort Lewis, WA], waiting for them to give the word for us to get on the plane to start our journey. Last night I didn't go to sleep until around 24:00 and wake up was at 01:00. I didn't get much sleep but I kind of did that on purpose so I would sleep more on the plane. The other part was because half the females were being goofy as hell. Two of the girls got in just their LBVs [Load Bearing Vest] and underwear and were about to go run around outside. I could not stop laughing.[1]

I am now on the plane. It has been a hard last two hours. I called mom and said my goodbyes. It

---

1. "I kind of did that on purpose …" ~ I kind of was scared out of my mind and looking to escape my thoughts through an abundance of alcohol. The women who ran around in their LBVs and undies were two of the mom aged women in the company. I see now, intentionally or not, they were preoccupying our worried minds with fun and laughter. Humor is often used as a protective mechanism by military. We're all jokesters until you peel back a few layers.

was probably the hardest thing I've ever had to do. I tried to stay strong and not cry but I couldn't help myself and of course that made matters worse because she started to cry.[2]

I just spoke to my sister. I woke her up. I'm so happy that she answered her phone. I would have been so sad if I wouldn't have been able to talk to her. That was really hard too because she started to cry almost right away. I love them so much and I hate it so much that I have to be away from them for so long.

---

2. At the age of 19 and getting ready to embark on one of the most difficult chapters of my life, I had already denied myself my true feelings. A not so great quality I leverage often in the entries to come.

May 4, 2003

Over in the United States it is still May 3rd but now that I am in Germany, it is May 4th. It's 22:26 in the U.S., where I am, it's 07:26. My mind and body are all messed up. I don't know what day it is or what time it is.

I spoke to my mom and sister again. It was a good conversation with no crying. It's funny because I was telling her how the sun was coming up and she was telling me how she was just getting home from the restaurant and going to bed.

Anyway, I am here on the plane again. We got to get off for a couple of hours and now we are on our way to Iraq. And what's funny is we don't know what our mission is or who we are attached to or where we will be staying.[3]

We just lifted off the air strip and I got my first

---

3. Flexibility is a must in the military. Plans change often. Not passing down all the information received now makes sense to me. It leaves less room for frustrated and pissed off soldiers.

good look at Germany. It is beautiful. The houses look like castles, and everything is so green. Well, we are about to eat breakfast and then I'm getting my hair braided, so until then …

We just landed in Kuwait, and I am feeling a little lightheaded. I can't believe we are here. It's 100° outside, something that I have been missing and I will have to get used to.

The plane is really quiet while we wait to unload. I think everyone else is a little freaked out, too.

I'm sitting here in our "holding area", which is basically a big ass tent with plywood as a floor. It looks as if we are going to be here for about a week. It's not that bad here. We have showers and a TV area and a phone center. As soon as we can, I am going to call my mom and sister.

And when I was at the chow hall, I saw a bunch of 82nd airborne and I asked them if their MPs were here. They are here and my new mission is to find them because John Radick is here. I will be so happy if I see him. Well hopefully we will get the word soon on when we can go take showers, so until then …

The day is now over and I'm about ready for bed. The word is that we won't be here much longer but the place we are going won't be much better. I guess that I'll just have to take it one day at a time.

May 5, 2003

Another day in paradise ... It has got to be at least 100° outside and I am loving it. I never want to go back to a cold place again.[4] So far today, we have done a whole lot of nothing. I woke up around 05:30. I couldn't sleep anymore, got dressed and ate chow. Then Petros and I were playing catch with the football a little later on. Then I got yelled at by SFC Moore because I was late for our accountability formation. I am so sorry that my watch was 10 minutes off his. Everyone is so uptight. I mean I know that we are in Kuwait but shit ... We are going to go stir-crazy. I just don't want to say anything anymore. I am going to become the silent bitch.[5]

---

4. Ha! I can't help but laugh. I moved to Montana in 2015. Montana has four to six month long winters and subzero temperatures.

5. I was very stubborn at a young age and clearly thought I knew best. I understand now that my leadership was simply preparing me for a world to come. Being prompt left little room for mistake and navigating with your team meant security. Little mistakes and security kept people alive. I get anxious today if I'm running late or believe I won't be on time. Deep

Then they have it to where you can't go anywhere without your whole fire team, which is just ridiculous. That means I have to get three other people to go with me to the bathroom and everything. But that's 72nd for ya. I got really close to finding John today but nothing so far. █████████████████████████

██

█████████████████████████ I hope I do.

Wow it has only been like 2.5 days, and we have moved already. We are now at a different camp. It's a lot better. I'll tell more tomorrow, I'm off to bed.

down I still believe my life, as well as other's, are at risk otherwise. "If you're not early, you're late", is often expressed in the military. At 19, I didn't fully comprehend that being early allowed the ability for further assessment, planning, and adjustment if necessary. All things I appreciate today. Although, I could do without the unsolicited stress.

May 6, 2003

So the word is that we will be leaving in approximately six days to the Baghdad International Airport. I think that once we get there, things won't be so bad. We will be working 12 hours days and no one will really have time to bicker. The thing that scares me is the three day drive up there.

We had a briefing today and they were talking about how when the convoys travel up North, there are people throwing rocks and stuff and trying to take stuff out of the vehicles. That scares me so bad. All I think about is that convoy that went up that way and got ambushed. I know that things have settled down a lot but there are still snipers and demonstrators out there who hate us and want us dead. I guess that I'll just have to take one day at a time.

I really want to talk to my mom and let her know that I am alright. I think that I might just write her because I was told that it is like a two-hour wait for the phone and you need a calling card, which I would have to wait another hour or so to get from the PX. I would be more than happy to do so, except that now there is a policy that during the day we have to have our whole fire team with us wherever we go and at night I have to have a male with me. I doubt that I could get those guys to go with me.

I really think that when I get home I will go active duty so I can be with a real "support" chain of command and have a real training with up-to-date equipment. Because for real—the National, now International, Guard is a joke, and my unit is a joke. I guess you just have to learn from your mistakes and grow.[6]

---

6. I sound so angry and frustrated. Just wait, Dallas. We're just getting warmed up. With that said, there was plenty to be upset with. We were very much under equipped, could have definitely used some more training, and in my opinion had some less than confident leadership. But that's the case in any organization. I've learned a lot of valuable lessons from people on behaviors I've chosen not to repeat.

May 7, 2003

Starting tomorrow, our company will be working the gates here at wonderful Camp Arifjan—yeah right. We will be working them until our equipment comes in, which should be around the 12th of May.[7] Then we'll be forwarded to Baghdad. I'm finally starting to get used to the time change. Eleven hour difference is pretty hard to get used to.

I tried to call home again today and again I have the worst luck because the stupid phones won't go through to Camp Doha. All you get is a busy signal. I could have talked to Mom and Kaylie twice now.[8] God this place bites.

---

7. When we left Fort Lewis, WA all of our equipment was packed into CONEX containers and put on a ship to be transported to Kuwait. I'm unsure whether they are first put on a train to the east coast or if they ship out from a west coast port.

8. When you call out, you are actually calling into a military installation and then being routed to another military installation, usually one that is closest to where you are calling. Often times the lines were busy at one or another. I visualize it similarly to the old telephone switch boards. Unplugging one line to connect to another, with limited wires.

May 8, 2003

Another day another dollar. Today has been a pretty relaxed day. Some of us went down to the MWR [Morale Welfare and Recreation] and watched the movie, *Darkness Falls* and then we came back and took a nap.

At 15:45, a one star general came by and spoke to us about our mission and gave us a little reassurance speech. General Hills was his name. He seemed like a good guy who was very much for his troops.

Last night I finally got in touch with Mom. It was so nice to hear her voice. And I know that it relieved her to hear mine.

Andy and I plan on staying up most of the night to get our clock ready for Friday's work, so I'll probably call home again. I am thinking about calling Eric tonight as well. I really want to fix things between us before we head up North, at least our friendship.

I have written quite a few letters in the last day. Mom, my brothers, Jason, Aunt Glenna, Dana. I figure that the more I write, my chances of getting mail back will be more likely. Which will help me out in the long run.[9]

I have promised to be on my very best behavior and to control my opinions so that I can get promoted. Basically they are asking me to be someone I'm not. ███████████████ certain way for so long and have established who you are, it is so hard to change and control yourself into being someone you're not. ████████████████████████████████ ████████████████████████████████ ████████████[10]

We got our first warning order this evening. It turns out that we have a mission to go to a city in North Iraq to pick up around 1,000 Iranian Nationals and take them to Tilia which is south of Baghdad. Most of them are women and children. We are not sure what platoon will be going, all we know is that it will be in the next couple of days and all the females are going. I am actually really excited to do this mission, it's actually positive.

Then after that we will be probably meeting the

---

9. What so many don't understand is how valuable a letter is to a soldier. I didn't even truly understand it's significance yet.

10. Again with my stubbornness. I'm happy to report that 20 years later, I have embraced many of the concepts that I initially rejected.

rest of our company in Baghdad to carry out the rest of our mission. The real cool thing is that we get to fly up there in a Chinook. I guess that we will find out more tomorrow.

May 10, 2003

Today has been a really short day, but a very informed one. I stayed up all night last night because I thought that I would be working tonight, but that changed. So, I slept all day and now it is 02:45 and I am still awake and not very tired.

I tried to call home and ended up leaving a message. ███████████████████████████████

So it looks as if we are leaving tomorrow afternoon. They took all our magazines and filled them with live ammo today and I have all my shit packed except the essentials. I guess it's going to be first platoon and six additional people from other platoons, four of them being female.

Andy opened up a lot to me today. He said a lot about his personal life that I feel privileged to know. I guess he trusts me, which is good because I trust him too. He's such a good guy. Well, I guess I will try to sleep now.

May 13, 2003

This morning I woke up on the side of a sand bunker next to the helicopter pad. We had all of our stuff packed and ready to go yesterday afternoon and we were loaded and transported down here at 22:00.[11] Now I sit here and wait for the word to jump on the Chinook and deploy to Baghdad International Airport. Finally, we are going. But there is still a question of what our mission will be when we get there.

We will either be doing escorting for the Iranian nationals or corrections for the prison. Either way we are finally here and finally going to start this deployment.

---

11. I had two bags. Every possession I had in two bags. Both of which I had to carry. My rucksack must have weighed close to 80 pounds and the second bag, somewhere around 50. I was 5'4" and 135 pounds and responsible for carrying my own belongings. This was rough and I'm still thankful for my 6+ foot, 230 pound team member that helped me out more than once. I remember walking to the Chinook and stumbling. He lifted all of me, and what I was carrying, up by the handle on top of my ruck to help stabilize me and get me to the helicopter.

I actually feel really privileged to do what I am doing.[12] My platoon in my company is the first of the Nevadans to step foot up there. Our company commander is going to email the state and let them know what we are going to be doing. So our story will probably be in the Review Journal. Hopefully mom will get that one.

This is a day that I will never forget. The day I go to defend my country and give peace to the Iraqis.[13]

---

12. I was also scared out of my mind. So scared, that I couldn't even write it down; that would have been accepting the fear. At that time, I needed pride. I needed courage.

13. When we landed in Baghdad, there was no one. The two Chinooks landed, we got out, grabbed our things, the Chinooks left, and there was no one around. The lieutenant (LT) had us pull a 360 degree security and after a few minutes, he and two others marched off as we were instructed to stay put. I'm not sure how long they were gone. It felt like forever as I laid in the prone position in the hot sun. Waiting. Waiting for what, I have no idea. He came back with what I could only describe as a garbage truck. He told us to load up and away we went. LT definitely always took care of us, and I was always thankful for his calvary background. Shoot. Move. Communicate. That was our platoon motto.

May 14, 2003

Here I sit in a tent with the rest of my platoon in a camp about one hour from downtown Baghdad. This camp that we are staged in used to be a camp for the Republican guard. We are now living in, bathing, and eating in a place where soldiers that once plotted against us used to live.[14]

We were looking in one of the buildings that had been blown up and there were all kinds of journals and log books and instructional books and newspapers all over the floor. I confiscated what looks like a history book. It would be so cool to bring home.[15]

We have showers but can only shower every

---

14. My squad, plus a few, were in one large tent, all lined up with cots and our belongings. I remember looking to my right and left thinking, well at least I'm safe. These men were the most secure thing I had in my life ever and we just happened to be in one of the most dangerous places ever. This day was also Andy's birthday. We celebrated with an MRE brownie and a match as a candle, all while in complete disbelief of where we were.

15. I indeed brought it home and have it still today.

three days, which is way better than none. We get one hot meal a day. The rest of the time it's MREs.

It took us three hours to fly here on Chinooks, which I got really sick on. I thought I was going to puke. Thank goodness I didn't.[16]

They are saying that we will start working at the prison in downtown Baghdad in about three days. Lieutenant (LT) says that he is going to try and make it so that we only have to work eight hour shifts. But then you have to add on the prep time and the hour drive there and back. So at least we will have 11 hour days, which is not bad at all.

---

16. This ride definitely solidified my motion sickness for me. I must have swallowed down puke at least three times before I passed out asleep with my head between my knees. I woke up just before we landed and realized I wasn't the only one, but at least I kept mine down.

May 15, 2003

Some of our guys went to downtown Baghdad yesterday and again today. They said it is pretty crazy down there. There are little kids and others running around everywhere asking military personnel for food. It's kind of sad, but I would have to say that we are doing our best.

There is a prison, a small one, up by us that is holding around 500 prisoners. Yesterday, a small riot broke out and they had my squad standby QRF [quick reaction force]. The riot broke up and calmed down by the time we got there, which is a good thing.

Then last night Petros, Perry, and I were down talking to a Sergeant McBird, I guess they know him from DLI [Defense Language Institute]. He is running the operation over there.

While we were there one of the prisoners got a little rowdy and the MPs slammed him. It was the most action that I have seen in three months. It is so crazy to look at that prison and to realize that this is not just another training exercise, it's real life and these are real criminals.[17]

Sergeant McBird said that about 85% of the prisoners don't really belong there, they were arrested for mostly petty shit like looting. But there are some guys in there for murder and rape.

Last night while we were asleep, a wildcat came up to our tent and four of our guys freaked out and started throwing rocks at it. It was so funny.

Earlier today Meyers and some others were out looking around and they came across the bones from human bodies. We were told that there are probably bodies under these blown up buildings that haven't been recovered yet. They also said they had seen a wild dog running around with a human hand in its mouth. God I hope I don't see anything like that.[18]

Alright! Yes! I just got the best detail in the world! Yeah right … I just got tasked out to go burn everyone's shit. Literally. That was the grossest thing I have ever done in my life. I about gagged five times. I guess that's what you get when you are

17. In the first few months, I often found myself teetering in confusion of reality and a dreamlike state of mind, having to take a step back and remind myself that this was not training. This was as real as it comes and to not let my guard down.

18. Unfortunately, I did see a dog with a hand and part of an arm roaming around. There were mass graves, what felt like, everywhere.

one of the lowest ranking personnel in your company.[19]

_____

19. Sgt. Lauren and I were tasked together. I have a picture of him posing with the stir stick on this day. This is a smell that stays with you. Not just physically—talk about praying it was your day to shower if you were handed this detail. It stays with you mentally too. The sheer mention of the task will have veterans gagging. Lauren took his own life in 2017. It was shared that he struggled with PTSD long before this deployment and long after. He was always kind to me and loved to talk about fast cars. We had so many intellectual conversations and I'm thankful to have known him and only wish I could have done something to help pull him out of the darkness he felt. A darkness I would come to know all too well myself one day.

May 18, 2003

The last 24 hours I have been so tired! My squad got up at 05:00 and started work at 06:00 in the prison. I guess the first two hours were just getting used to being around all of the prisoners. We had to escort them to the bathroom, to get water, and to take their trash out. Then we had head count, where we had to go inside each of the cells — there are nine of them — and form them in 10 formations and write down each of their wristband numbers.

Then admin calculates to make sure everyone is there. During this process, everyone is on lockdown. While we count heads we also go into the tents and basically tear everything apart and make sure there are no weapons that got smuggled in. Then it's back to escort here and there. So we thought at least...

There I was watching about 30 new prisoners waiting to get processed with two other MPs and a riot breaks out in Charlie [C] cell. So they called QRF, and they came and pointed out the "ringleader." They moved in to grab him, which was successful until they were leaving the cell. That's when some of the inmates started grabbing and pulling on the MPs. The MPs made it out of the cell but once they did, the prisoners started throwing big rocks and took some of their tent down and were using the poles to hit us. Then in the same minute I heard a gun go off.

Right about now my heart is going a million miles an hour. And here I am still on watch of 30 brand new prisoners, who all are looking at me. And in return I'm looking at them, thinking to myself that if any of these guys try to make a move, I am going to grab this pole next to me and start swinging.

About five minutes later, things start to calm down and all the prisoners I am watching stand fast, lucky for them. It turns out that things just went crazy over there and the gun shot was supposed to be a warning shot. In reality, it ricocheted and shot an inmate in the arm.

Numerous MPs got hit with the rocks, including one of our guys. But in all reality things didn't get too out of hand. No MPs got badly injured, and no inmates escaped. Really, we had everything under control. The whole place was surrounded by SAWs [Semi-Automatic Weapon].[20]

After that, things went back to normal, and I actually started to feel a little more comfortable working around the prisoners. I learned a couple phrases that help me communicate with them. Just the basics like: be quiet, sit down, stop.[21]

They are switching out the squads every day. So every third day I'll be working out there.

---

20. Honestly, this was a chaotic event where a lot could have gone wrong. Those prisoners could have easily taken over that facility. We were lucky most were amateur criminals.

21. It was very helpful to know some of the language. I wish this would have been a part of our initial training prior to leaving the States.

May 21, 2003

Wow, have we been busy. The 19th we went out to the prison in downtown Baghdad. We pulled security for the engineers on the way there, while they worked, and on the way back. It was a long day.

This prison out there is literally a dump. There's trash and pieces of God knows what piled everywhere. They are expecting to have this prison up and running within a week or so. I really don't think that is going to happen. It is going to take a lot to get this place looking like it's ready to be ran.

We found out today that we are moving over there to live tomorrow. That should be interesting considering there is no running water, established toilets, or any kind of electricity.[22]

---

22. I remember driving in on Humvees seeing 15-foot-high mounds of trash and rabid dogs roaming similarly to hyenas preying on the remains of whatever they might find. The buildings were worn, some barely standing. Walls were missing, looking as though they had been blown out with force from the outside. The inmate cells looked like there was a mass jail break and a mad dash to get as far away as possible. There were still shallow tubs

Andy and I think the only good thing is that we won't be living inside a tent anymore. We will be in a building. Well besides the fact that all the windows have been blown out, we might stay cool.

Another major factor is that the area is not secured by any infantry so we will be pulling 24 hour security on the whole compound. Needless to say, we won't be getting much sleep. And it doesn't help that there is a small village right next to it full of people.[23]

Yesterday was Mom's birthday. I wish I could have told her happy birthday. Instead I worked the EPW [Enemy Prisoner of War] compound. Nothing out of control happened. It was just really hot. I think the hottest it has been since we have been here. There were inmates dropping everywhere from dehydration. I believe one of the older inmates may have died. Last I know, he was getting CPR.

So today is like the only day that my squad has really had off. It is nice to be able to relax even

---

that looked to be used for washing the abandoned clothes sitting next to the chamber pots and empty cigarette packs. The smell was a combination of death and shit. One that would become all too familiar.

23. This is a very large facility, 280 acres, with roughly 120 soldiers getting ready to occupy it. That of which only 60 or so could be pulling security at any given time. The rest were a part of the headquarters (admin, supply, mechanic, chemical), officers, and high ranking enlisted (NCOs). Now also take into consideration we would be responsible for setting up the prison, intaking prisoners, supporting convoy missions for supplies, and oh yeah sleep.

though it's 100+ degrees outside. We can't really catch up on sleep, it's way too hot. All you do is sit there and sweat balls.[24]

---

24. By "sweat balls," I mean lay on your cot in a pool of your own sweat constantly being added to by every pore on your body.

May 24, 2003

Alright, I am going to stop saying that things could be worse because every time I say that they get worse. I am now living in an old prison in Baghdad. This place is like a trash dump with buildings. There is a big yard where we will be keeping the prisoners. We are supposed to be getting 300 prisoners, give or take, tomorrow morning. And we still have a shit load of stuff we need to do before this can be a livable environment, even for the hajis[25] to be in.

We moved in last night and slept in the alleyway between two warehouses. One of which we will soon be living in. I do have to say it will be a whole lot cooler and we will have a lot more room than any other place we have been so far. I had some difficulty falling asleep last night. Just about

---

25. Haji is a term often used by the U.S. military to refer to all Iraqi people. I was uneducated at the time and went with what everyone else was using. The term actually refers to a Muslim who has been to Mecca as a pilgrim.

every five minutes there would be gunfire going off. I finally just put on my headphones, turned up my music, and fell asleep.[26]

Everyone woke up around 01:00 freezing their asses off. It got really cold this morning. It felt so good. I had duty this morning from 09:00 to 12:00 at the ECP [entry control point]. Being out in the sun for three hours really wore me out.

The battalion's command sergeant major came through. He had some civilian with him. I'm still wondering why they are here.

The engineers finally showed up. They are cleaning out the warehouse we will be living in. Hopefully I can hide long enough that I don't get tasked to lay wire for the camp.[27] We'll see how long that lasts.

---

26. I can't help to laugh at myself. Clearly I was not thinking with my logical brain and was prioritizing sleep over safety. I do not advise putting in headphones or earplugs in a combat zone to drown out the sound of gunfire. (Sigh)

27. Laying wire entailed pounding t-posts into the ground and then stacking and securing concertina wire in a triangle, forming the boundaries of what would become the EPW camp.

May 25, 2003

So early with nothing to do. Woke up this morning at 05:00 to get ready to go to work at the jail only to find out I am staying behind. I guess they only needed six people. Either that or some others from another platoon are going. I kind of wanted to go, though. At the jail is where all the high priced criminals are. Saddam's nephew is supposed to be there, and I think "Chemical Ali" too.[28] Oh well, I guess I'll just get to stay here and play platoon bitch.[29]

The 200 prisoners are supposed to come in today. I hope that we are all set up enough for them. I believe that they are coming from the EPW camp.

---

28. Chemical Ali is a nickname for Ali Hassan Abd al-Maid al-Tikriti. (I know, a mouthful!) He was an Iraqi politician and military commander under Sadam Hussein. He was also Sadam's first cousin. The nickname was given to him by Iraqi's for his use of chemical weapons in the attacks against the Kurds.

29. Platoon Bitch: person tasked with miscellaneous, most likely undesirable, tasks that seem to be never ending.

Those guys are sometimes a handful. But I don't think they will get away with too much here. It seems as if when 72nd is in control, full control, we run our facilities like we are gods and nothing can stand in our way. So I think we will do all right. [30]

We moved into the warehouse last night. I have probably 7 feet by 7 feet of room to myself. It's great.[31] On two sides I have it blocked off with my poncho and poncho liner. I even made some shelves out of three boxes. Goodness, sometimes I can be so creative.[32]

---

30. This day is referenced as an achievement in one of my recommendations for award writeups, ultimately leading to one of my two ARCOM (Army Commendation) medals. Although it references the opening of the Al Saliyah Jail and my contributions to that mission. This is the name of the jail in downtown Baghdad I would travel to.

31. Dear Dallas, please try to remember at one point in your life, you were extremely grateful for just 49 square feet.

32. And resourceful! A quality I hold dear still today. If it wasn't for the military's lack of resources, I may have never embraced my mad Macgyver skills.

May 26, 2003

Today has been a tiring day and it has just started. I woke up at 09:00 and started working outside on the EPW camp laying wire and pounding poles.[33]

Today is the first day that I actually got sun-burned. Mostly my shoulders. It hurts, too. Usually I am really good about putting on sunblock.

So we got done with the compound and I ran outside to hurry and wash my DCUs [Desert Combat Uniform] and hope they dry in time. My squad has to work tonight from 20:00 to 08:00 at

---

33. We (the 72nd MP Co.) built the EPW camp from the ground up. When we weren't pulling security for our area, when we weren't providing security on convoy missions, when we weren't looking after prisoners, or trying to get a couple hours of sleep, we were pounding t-posts into the ground and laying concertina wire. Concertina wire is large, coiled razor wire that was typically stacked in threes forming a triangle and used as the perimeter of the EPW camp and cells. Even though we were at a prison, it had been destroyed during the initial invasion, mostly by the Iraqis. So, we built an external camp until the resources were available to have the prison operational. There were a lot of terrible things that happened at that place prior to the invasion and occupation. Some of the stories that were told by locals or etched into the walls of the solitary confinement cells were horrific.

the jail in the heart of Baghdad. Maybe I will be able to slip in a nap before I have to work. That is, if I can sleep in this heat.

I am here in the heart of Baghdad at the jail. It looks a lot like one of our county jails. Iraqi police that are here are really cool. They don't speak too much English but with hand gestures we communicate pretty well.

On our way here, there was a Humvee that got blown up by either an RPG [Rocket Propelled Grenade] or a mine. All four soldiers were medevac'd [medical evacuation by helicopter] to the hospital. I hope that they are alright. I don't think that it was an RPG, it's been too calm around that area for something like that. I think that they probably drifted off the road a little and hit a mine. The Humvee was all black.

I guess that all the prisoners here are just waiting for a trial and most of them are ones that deserve to be here — armed robbery, rape, murder, etc. Well I don't know how much longer I will last. I am so tired.

May 28, 2003

Well, here I am back at the jail working another 12-hour shift. We got off yesterday at 10:00 and on the way back to camp we had to take a detour because of the blown up Humvee and got a little lost. We ended up in what looked like a big outdoor swap meet. Anything you could think of buying was there on the street. There were so many people out. We had to keep our eyes wide open for any sign of sniper or hostile individual.[34]

We finally found our way back to the highway. There was a little bit of a backup and when we were stopped a bunch of kids crowded around. One had crystal blue eyes. I took a picture of all of them.[35]

---

34. This situation is the worse feeling. You don't know where to have your eyes focus. Another situation that could have ended very badly but, by the grace of God, didn't.

35. I remember having such an emotional conflict internally seeing these children. They were cute and seemed very kind and genuinely curious. On the other hand, I knew there had been several encounters of children and women strapping bombs to their bodies, willing to be martyrs. To look at

When we finally made it back I passed out on my cot. I had only slept three hours of the last 32. I woke up this morning at 05:00, only to start all over again.

We were an hour late for work because our squad leader got us all lost at the detour again. Only this time it was much worse. We were out in the BFE. God only knows how we found our way.[36]

The kid who lives in the apartment building across the street — we called him Smiley[37] — went to get all of us hamburgers. I am looking forward to that. Although I am not so sure that the meat is cow, but I am going to try not to think about that and just enjoy my lunch.[38]

---

children in such a suspicious way and be willing to kill them is quite the mind fuck, especially as a woman who's every inclination is to embrace and nurture these young souls.

36. I couldn't believe we put ourselves in this situation again. The look of panic consumed my team leader's face. I can see it as clearly as if he were standing in front of me now. However, that didn't overcome him. He calmly and confidently relied on the resources we had - like a map - and got us back on track. He left a wife and daughters at home. I thought about them often, grateful for them to lend him to me for this deployment. My team leader was a solid leader that always made me feel secure and confident.

37 Smiley had the most beautiful and contagious smile. One that opened from ear to ear. He was so kind, curious, intelligent, and giving. He must have been around 15 years old. He hung out with us most days we were there, telling us stories of what it was like before and during the initial invasion. I wish I would have learned his real name and I only pray he is thriving today.

38. The meat ended up to be goat. It was good. Or I was hungry. Or just done eating MREs. Or a combination of all or some.

May 30, 2003

The 29th of May does not really exist to me. It was just one big blur. I woke up and felt sick, so I walked out by the bathrooms[39] and started puking until I was dry heaving.

Someone found me and brought me to the doctor. He laid me down, put an IV in me and also gave me a shot of something. It made me feel re-

---

39. "Bathrooms" is such a conservative word to use. I feel obligated to elaborate on what our bathrooms were before and at this point. Imagine a three feet deep trench dug into the ground in one straight line about a football field length long. Now construct a three feet tall box with no roof and a one foot diameter circle cut out of the bottom and place it on top of the trench. Line several of these boxes up along the ditch three or four feet apart. That was the "bathroom" at the first camp I was at. Everyone lined up, pretending they couldn't see, smell, or hear the person to the left or right of them while trying to handle their business as quickly as possible. At the prison, we also had a trench, but only about 50 feet long with two six-foot tall plywood boxes hovering over top. Within the box was another box with a circle cut out of the top - similar to a toilet - containing the bottom third of a metal barrel inside. Everyone shit in it and when they got full (or you couldn't enter the box without dry heaving anymore) we removed the barrel, poured diesel fuel atop, and burned it. This is why I say "I walked over BY the bathrooms". Not to or in the bathroom.

ally weird. I felt drunk and drowsy but jittery and cracked out at the same time. I didn't like it at all.

When I was done with the bag, they brought me back to my cot and I tried to go back to sleep but like every 10 minutes I would wake up jumpy.

While I was sleeping, I missed a lot. A riot broke out here at our prison. One of the guard towers claimed that they were fired upon.[40] And at the jail, the prisoners broke out of one of their cells. A bunch of madness happened. But the good thing is, every situation was brought back under control.

So I pretty much have the day off, that's if they don't find a detail for me. Hopefully they will just let me rest so that I can get over whatever I may have. Doc says that I probably caught something that made me sick. Then from puking, I dehydrated myself. So I'll rest and start back to work tomorrow at 07:00 at the jail.[41]

---

40. I only say "claimed" because quite frankly there was always gunfire going off and sometimes it would ricochet towards us. Up to this point some of us were on edge and some of us were in complete disbelief that anyone would fire at us. I was in disbelief. After all, I'd already been in some pretty risky situations, and no one fired. I felt like the longer I remained in this mindset, the better our chances were of not being directly shot at. This was also irresponsible of me. Awareness is key to survival.

41. I find it hilarious that I didn't relate my being sick to the fact that I ate an unknown meat, stored, and cooked in unknown conditions, served to me by a teenage boy of whom I only knew by a name we gave him (most likely because we couldn't pronounce his name) for a very short time. Yep, must have just been a "bug" I caught.

May 31, 2003

Here I am again sitting at the jail. Today is supposed to be the last day here. They are moving the last of the prisoners here to Camp Cropper and then we are moving to another jail that is going to be empty. Why we will be there I couldn't tell you. Your guess is as good as mine. Maybe they will move prisoners there. I hope that is not too far from where we are now. We have the hook ups here.

I had forgotten to mention that the other night, I believe the 28th, Petros and I ██████████ ████████████████████ We got off at 19:00 so Petros, Andy and I ████████████████ ████████████ Nothing much though. ███████████████████████████████████ Then ████████████████████████████████████ ███████████████████████ Tonight will probably be a rerun of last. Petros ████████

I had one of the guards write my full name in Arabic. It looks something like this:

I think that it is pretty neat to see my name transfer to another language.[42] So I sit here as Andy is plucking Smiley's eyebrows. Smiley is looking at us like Andy is nuts. I don't think he has ever seen or heard of anything of the sort.[43]

---

42. Okay, let's think about this. Dallas, translated into Arabic. Less than likely. Someone who can read Arabic, please tell me what he wrote.

43. Listen, we did any and all things to take our minds off of our current situation or to make us feel a little piece of home. Don't judge.

June 2, 2003

I cannot believe that it is June already. Hopefully time will keep flying like this. A lot has happened today. This morning I woke up at 05:00 to go with first squad to the jail to meet my squad so that I could go with them to use the phone. I called Mom and Kaylie and got to talk to the both of them. It was so nice to hear their voices. I got really teary-eyed, but in a happy way. I felt so much better. They were really surprised to hear my voice. They were glad. After that we came back to camp and went outside and worked on the compound some more.

Then when we got done, I was walking inside and saw a bunch of people crowding around Blue's cot. So I went over there, and it looked as if he was having a seizure. I was so scared for him, and I started to cry.

We ended up having to take him to the Third Infantry Division's hospital to see a doctor. We almost had him medevac'd out. But the nurse here got him calmed down and a little more stable, so we just drove.

The doctor there said that it was a combination of heat cramps and heat exhaustion but could be more. By the time we left him, he had gone through four IVs, had a catheter inserted, and had been poked and prodded in places he will be pissed about later.

The doctor told us to come back in about three hours to check on him and maybe take him back. So we did, but the doctor said that they wanted to hold him overnight so that they could further consult him. I guess that was because he may have gotten something viral and wanted to make sure.

Sgt Moore went in to check on him. They wouldn't let me, and he said that Blue was looking a little better and was starting to come to. I guess he didn't know what was going on at all. His exact words were "what the fuck?" He is said to be all right and that he will be coming back tomorrow morning. Sure hope so. He scared me so badly today. I said prayers all day.

The new rumor going around now is that we are going to be moving again. We will be over by the airport in tent city. I am told that the tents will have plywood floors so we won't be in the dirt and there is a possibility they might be air-conditioned.

(I doubt it.) I have heard there are showers[44] set up over there as well. It will be good to get out of this trash dump of a hell hole. God I just hate moving. I have moved nine times in the last three months. I also think that in the tent we won't have too much room. Which will suck. It is kind of nice having your own little space.

Petros got moved out of our squad and platoon today. They moved her to third platoon. I hope that they don't think that this is going to solve all the problems. It only solved one and that is Petros's.[45] I wish I was only as lucky as she. She is in Sgt Mat's team, in Sgt Pearson's squad, in Sgt Red's Platoon. That is a great chain of command. Hopefully things will get better with time. Just not too much I hope.

---

44. Let's talk about the shower situation at the prison. There isn't one. We kept ourselves clean with baby wipes. At some point, one of the females was sent a camping shower bag. One you fill with water, lay in the sun to heat, and then hang to use. We found an empty room in the prison, most likely once used for an office, and took turns standing on a crate holding the bag up for the other to use. Eventually we finagled a way to hang it and could have three minutes of cleansing privacy every 7-10 days. Keep in mind that we had no running water and were rationed drinking water. It was a huge sacrifice of drinking water to be used to bathe. And the fact that we were put in a position to even make that choice is astonishing to me today. Honestly, I get emotional thinking about it. I'm sad for that 19 year old girl and humbled 20 years later.

45. I don't remember all the details of what was going on with Petros. Even if I did, that would be her story to share. What I can say is she felt uncomfortable and the move was to resolve that feeling.

June 3, 2003

There were some things that I had forgotten to mention last night, and I woke up this morning remembering them. Like after we had gone and checked on Blue to maybe bring him back, we were driving back and only about five minutes away from the camp, both of our trucks heard gunfire go off and we were pretty convinced that it was being directed towards us. So we sped out of there. We reported it to the first sergeant, and he passed it up as well. The next thing we know there are two Apache gunships flying around and pretty low. I guess that they were scouting out the area that was reported to be fire. Green, Wagner, and I got on one of the roofs and took pictures. I think they will be pretty awesome.[46] I also think that they were showing off a little towards the end of their mission

---

46. This picture did turn out to be awesome. So awesome that it was made into our deployment coin.

because they were flying directly above us, low, and sidewinding it. It was cool.

Also when Petros told me about her moving to third platoon, I remember that I had a dream the night prior. In my dream, Petros and I were having a meeting with our chain of command, and they told Petros that she was moving to third platoon. Teal was going to be her squad leader. Which is the only part that doesn't go because Teal is only an E4. But that could have just meant he may be one someday.

Well, this morning Blue is supposed to be picked up, but I don't see it happening soon. There are a lot of other missions that have been put out and no Humvees[47] left. I really hope he's alright.

I have to work outside on the compound again today whenever third squad is done with their extra tasks. Then hopefully I will be able to get a few hours of sleep before I have to go to work with my squad tonight at the jail. They boosted the count of MPs up to being present at the jail now and since our squad only has eight now that Petros is gone

---

47. Let's chat about our Humvee situation, shall we? We were driving softshell Humvees. Zero armor. We had taken the doors off to broaden our view and mobility. It's not like they would shield us from anything anyhow. One of the Humvees, that more or less resembled a truck, had been manipulated by our mechanic with a tripod that could hold a 50 caliber rifle or a M249. So we drove really fast and defensive while shooting first and asking questions later.

and Blue is sick I have to work and they will have to grab someone from third squad as well.

Alright, well I am going to lay down and relax before I have to go to work out in the hot sun.

Well I was woken up to go to work as well as to find out that Blue is still not better and that they medevac'd him to someplace in southern Iraq where he can receive full medical treatment. They said that his temperature wasn't going down among other things. They seem to think that he caught some kind of an Iraqi bug that just made everything a whole lot worse. I pray to God that he recovers from this. Maybe they will send him home so that way he can get all the medical treatment he needs, plus he will get to be with his family. I wonder if anyone has contacted his mom. I wish they would just let me call her. She would probably take it better if it came from me and not Red Cross.

You know, it still really upsets me that McGill seems to not give a shit about what is happening to Blue. When he was tripping at camp, he didn't even get up to help with anything. I just don't understand how he can say he is his friend and then turn around and do this shit. I know for a fact that if anything would have happened to him, Blue would be concerned. He has already shown it. Maybe through this he will realize that he is really not his friend. It's all right though, because he has Maze and me and we will always be there, no matter what.

June 5, 2003

I just woke up at the jail. I stayed up as long as I could before I crashed. And it didn't help that ███████████████████████████████████ So here I am back at the jail again. I feel like I never leave this godforsaken place. I might as well just move in.

This morning when we went back to the camp, I went right to sleep. Then I woke to the sound of Blue's voice. I was looking around and didn't see him. I thought I was just dreaming. Then I saw him and told him to come here, and I gave him the biggest hug and started to cry with so much happiness. It was so great to see him and know for myself that he was all right. He said that he had a minor heart attack and that the doctors aren't too sure what caused it besides stress and lack of sleep. If that is the case, everyone in the company will probably be having heart attacks. They work us to death.[48]

---

48. We truly did work a lot, slept very little, and had minimal nutrition while being rationed water. Most days at this point we were getting two to three hours of sleep at most here and there. I remember many times hanging half out the Humvee on the way to the jail in town, nodding off, begging myself to stay awake, and keep my eyes open, for my own safety. It was often a losing battle. I have no idea how we operated this way for so many months and survived.

June 6, 2003

Here I am at my home away from home away from home, the jail. It is a very quiet night. Almost the whole squad is asleep. I think that I would have been too if I wouldn't have slept all day and drank like six sodas tonight. I feel like I am watching the rerun of the TV show that no one likes because they have seen it way too many times. Every day it is the same thing.[49]

The only thing that happened differently today is that I ate a chicken and tomato sandwich from the market. It was really good. I almost felt like I was at home, not!!![50]

Every day I grow to hate this place more and more and I get more homesick day after day. I miss

---

49. How grateful I would come to be for those predictable, repetitive days and nights.

50. We were instructed to not eat any of the local food. We disobeyed these orders every chance we got. At this point a month worth of MREs and T-RATS were unbearable. The rotisserie chicken and fresh tomatoes were divine, or at least I thought so at the time.

my mom so much. I wish that I would get some of her mail she had sent to me. I find myself looking at her picture more often. It is like if I stare at it long enough, she might turn into life. But there she sits in the picture with the same expression on her face. I can't wait to go home.[51]

---

51. Sometimes I would find myself in such a trance that I would start to hallucinate. I'm sure that the lack of sleep and nutrition didn't help. I would see my mom's photo come to life. It lasted long enough for me to question my own sanity, shake it off, and then get back to whatever I should be doing.

June 9, 2003

Yesterday was the last day of working at the jail. I feel bad that I didn't get to say goodbye to Smiley. He gave me a beautiful silver necklace with a silver cross.[52] I wish I could have said thank you, since he gave it to Brown to give to me. I have to say that I will miss going down there. I learned a lot while working there.[53]

Today was my platoon's first day off since we have been out here. It was nice to relax a little bit. We did do a couple of small details but all in all it was a pretty smooth day.

----

52. I still have the necklace and can see Smiley's smile, ear to ear, every time I see it.

53. So many bittersweets. I hated the place, but truth is that mission got us out of the prison and allowed us to see and experience a little of what the country had to offer. The stories that were shared by the Iraqi guards were equally terrible and enlightening. They shared how Saddam and his leaders would have the family of those sentenced to death come to watch their execution. They were told to keep their eyes open or another of their family members would face the same fate. Saddam and his leaders would laugh while drinking whiskey. Apparently Saddam loved whiskey.

Tomorrow we start working the EPW compound with the other two platoons. Since there will be three platoons working now, our days have been cut down to eight hours. My platoon got a pretty good shift too. We will be working from 20:00 to 04:00. I know that sounds shitty, but we won't be working in the heat of the day at all. So that will be better for us. Less heat casualties.

The commander said that on the 15th of this month some guy is supposed to take this entire operation over and he will decide whether or not he wants to keep it running or not. I guess that there is a bunch of politics involved. If he desires not to, we may be going home a lot sooner than expected. But if he keeps it, then who knows when we will be leaving. I guess we will just have to wait and see.

June 11, 2003

I am sitting here in tower two on the perimeter of the prison pulling security. The 400th MP battalion completely took over the inside of the compound. I think that a little of that was decided based upon what had happened yesterday.

Everyone was woken up at 04:00 to learn that six prisoners had escaped, only one had been recaptured. They were all juveniles and the one recaptured was torn up from all of the wire that they had to crawl through. The only part of the camp that wasn't lit up with lights … they crawled through the wire and snuck around, found a ladder, propped it up against the wall and slid down the other side. By the time we were awake, dressed, and in our vehicles, they were long gone.

Then just as we were released from sweeping the area, got in bed, and had just fallen asleep, I was awoken again to a warning of a mortar attack. So my platoon rushed out in our Humvees and set up a perimeter approximately 500 meters away from the compound to look for any kind of suspicious acts. We sat out there for about 45 minutes and then were called into the base. We then found out that it had just been a battle drill. I was so mad that they did that because I was so scared. I asked my LT that since we had done a good job and passed the test, could we go home now? He laughed. But I wasn't joking.

So by this time it was around 13:00 and I crawled into my bed hoping to sleep for a couple hours before we went on shift at 20:00. Turns out, I got that and then some. My squad was on QRF, so we got to sleep a little. We got off at 04:00 and I slept until about 07:00, went on an escort mission for the commander, came back, and slept some more.

This time I awoke to Sgt Black walking towards me with mail in his hands. Three of the letters were for me. Two from my sister and one from my mom. Mail is really the best thing here. It's such a relief to hear from family and friends back home.[54] Read-

---

54. I'm not sure people truly understand the significance mail had on our mental health. Those of us that received mail lit up like a Christmas tree. Those that did not had instant looks of sadness and disappointment. Sometimes, I watched what started as happy faces transform into sadness, disappointment, and anger. I know of at least two of my fellow soldiers who received "Dear John letters". It was disgusting. Absolutely horrid. To know what they had sacrificed and were enduring, only to receive a letter calling off a marriage, asking for divorce, notified of cheating. Then for them to

ing my mom's letter almost brought me to tears. It was as if I could hear her reading the letter to me. I wonder when we will get to use the phone again. I hope soon.

---

lock that away, on top of all else, while being shot at or dealing with hostile individuals — just sick.

June 13, 2003

Friday the 13th, today has been cursed. I woke up
and went to the bathroom and when I came back
everyone was running around like chickens with
their heads cut off. I was like what the hell is going
on now. Sgt Mount told me that the headcount was
short, and they thought that a couple of prisoners
had escaped. So half of my platoon went to sweep
the outside of the compound and the other half, including myself, went and stood by for QRF. Things
settled down for about a half hour and then all hell
broke out again.

Oh and before they had miss counted, so no one
had escaped.

So this time the prisoners were going crazy. As I
am getting ready to go out there, I heard gunfire, so
I hurried up and came to find out that the prisoners
were throwing rocks and using tent poles as spears
to harm the MPs. So two of the towers shot up the

prisoners. Six of the prisoners were wounded and one died after we tried to revive him.

My squad and I were out clearing a landing strip for the medevac when he died. I know he did wrong, but it was really sad. He kept saying, "my babies, my babies." When the medic said that he was about to go, I left. I did not think that I could watch another person die, regardless of who it was. I think that it may have brought back bad memories.[55]

So the medevac came, and I took pictures of them landing while I was getting sandblasted. I don't think that the prisoners will act up for a while. Maybe that needed to happen. I know I'll sleep a little better tonight knowing they are scared.[56]

---

[55]. I lost (what might as well have been) my stepdad on Easter in 2001 to a lethal dune buggy accident. That was the first person I saw die. This was the second. Unfortunately, it would not be my last.

[56]. This day and event are referenced as an achievement in one of my recommendations for award writeups, ultimately leading to one of my two ARCOM (Army Commendation) medals.

June 14, 2003

Here I sit on tower number four. It looks directly over the compound, where prisoners had escaped before. I really don't think that they will pull that off again. We now have two Humvees with three personnel watching that side along with the roving guard and the three towers around the compound.

Today was a quiet day for the camp. I think that the prisoners got the point. Some say that will only last until most of the prisoners here now leave and new ones get recycled in.

Today on Fox News they talked about what had happened yesterday. But they forgot to mention what company was running the compound. I guess we aren't getting any credit.

Right now all of the prisoners are chanting and singing. It is actually really peaceful. I only wish that I could videotape it. It's very interesting.

My squad, as well as first, attempted to go to Camp Victory to use the phones today. I was really excited to be able to talk to my mom and sister. But they wouldn't allow us in. They said only people that live there, which is the Fifth Corps, and people with official business could enter. Everyone was pretty pissed. Hopefully the commander will find another place. I would hate to be here for a long time without being able to talk to family.

.

June 19, 2003

Four days ago, McGill was on tower two and had claimed he saw a head through his night vision. So QRF, along with some others, including myself, were sent out to clear the entire prison. It took about two hours and we found nothing. I think that it was probably some of our guys fucking around and when they heard we were going out to search, they ran back inside and never told anyone.

Then the next day somebody claimed that they heard Iraqis whispering so again the prison had to be searched. And again, nothing was found. People need to stop messing around.

Last night I was in tower one with Brown and we played a joke on the ECP. Brown went down from the tower and was throwing rocks at them. Then he went into a warehouse across from them and shined his flashlight a couple of times. They tripped and called up to me and asked if I had seen anything. I was laughing so hard. We finally told him we were just messing with them.[57]

Tonight I have QRF. Those nights used to be the relax shift, but not anymore. Now they have all this stupid shit we have to do. We have to man a Humvee out by tower seven and have one guy post by the showers and one by the wall in the front. All the shit happened since we had to clear the prison twice. Higher up is scared now that there might be someone still in here and they might sneak in and hurt them while they are having their precious sleep. Waaa. Oh well.

So I'm going to take a nap now before I have to go to work so maybe I won't fall asleep on duty.

---

57. I love how I criticize the possibility of people playing jokes around prisoners escaping and roaming the grounds but then do that very thing just days later. How quick I was to forget. Or bored.

June 20, 2003

Here I sit on tower one again, only this time with Rogers. If anyone was to see me right now, they would laugh their asses off. I am sitting here with my NVGs [Night Vision Goggles] on, trying to focus enough so that I can write. It is actually quite hard. But I am bored, so I figure I'll try just about anything to amuse myself.[58]

Today Andy went to Camp Cropper and ran into his "friend." It was very promising. I am happy for him. Maybe he'll get some. Because I know I'm not, but that's okay. I can wait until I get home.[59]

I wrote John a letter today. I hope it finds him. I opened up a lot in the letter and I hope he takes it seriously but not the wrong way.

---

58. I really do wish I had a photo of this. Or even better, video. NVGs aren't really meant for up close vision and work off reflective light. This made what I was seeing shadowed and blurry. Hence the short entry.

59. So many were on the hunt for a sexual release. Honestly, I found it gross. Everything was so dirty. Everyone was so dirty.

Andy got stuck with McGill tonight. I wonder how that's going. I guess I'll find out after shift.

June 26, 2003

As I sit here on tower two, I look out at the scenery, listening to the Iraqis praise Allah. Also in the background gunfire goes off like firecrackers on the Fourth of July. As the sun sets, I prep myself for another short eight hours, yet really long night.[60]

Tonight I am accompanied by Perrie. This will be my third night working with him. I enjoy his company. He is a great guy. I do find that the more you work with somebody, the less things you have to say to each other. And that is one thing that helps a lot when you are trying to stay awake close to the end of shift.[61]

---

60. The contrast of my senses was overwhelming at times and very confusing. I hear this beautiful song yet I hear gunfire. I see people in prayer but they'd also most likely slit my throat if given the opportunity.

61. Mostly because you've said everything you could ever say. It doesn't seem possible but most of us were relatively young and after you've spent 300-400 hours with someone…well, they pretty much know everything. Then the conversations turn to gossip or hypotheticals. The latter not being a good choice, often leading to anxious thoughts.

I received a package from grandma two days ago. It consisted of a couple of books, Kool-Aid, multi grain bars, baby wipes, and a couple other goodies. It was nice to finally get a package. Now all I would like is a letter from mom. We are supposed to be going to the phones tomorrow at 07:00. So by the time we get there and call, it will be around 21:00 at home. Hopefully mom will be home. If she is not, I'm not sure who I will call. ████████████ ████████████████████████ I'm not too sure though.

June 27, 2003

I am not too sure how to put this day into words, so I'll just start from the beginning and see where it goes. I woke up this morning at 07:00 with the intentions of going to the phone and calling mom. I was so happy. I always look forward to hearing her voice. There were no Humvees left to take, so we crawled into the back of two deuces[62]. Perrie drove one with Almeida as an A driver[63] with Halls, Mc-Gill, Daren, Hunt, James, Rogers and Wess in the back. Blue drove the other with Forder as the A driver with Mount, Barnes, and me in the back. We led the way. We pulled out of the prison and just outside we passed Carmen, Sgt Vernes, and some others coming in. We continued out of the external wall. I was thinking about what I was going to say

---

62. Deuce: a two and half ton, single cab, cargo truck. The bed was covered with a canopy, so those that were in the back of it couldn't be seen ... or see.

63. A Driver: supervisor or manager responsible for safely transporting cargo, troops, and providing advanced mobility on all missions.

to mom and tell her the things I wished for her to send, then it was as if I stepped inside a movie.

There was a very loud boom that I really didn't hear.[64] All that registered in my ears was a ringing sound and then came an instant headache. Simultaneously I looked towards the deuce behind us which was only about 50 meters behind. All I saw was a cloud of mixed black smoke and brown dust. I looked again and saw a body lying to the side. At the same time, Blue had sped up to get out of the kill zone. When he stopped, Sgt Mount, Barnes, and I jumped out of the back of the deuce and ran over to the other deuce while Blue and Forder pulled the deuce back around.

I automatically went to the 9 o'clock to pull security for whatever had just happened. On my way I noticed that the body I had seen lying off to the side was Rogers and there was some blood. At this point I was just trying to keep myself together and focus on my new mission, keeping my fellow soldiers safe from further attack.

It seemed like only seconds later we had realized that it had been a mine that had completely blown off the first set of dual tires on the passenger side of the truck. It only seems like minutes later

---

64. The sound was more felt than heard. Like the vibration and frequency shot through me and then again when it recoiled, almost simultaneously.

Humvees came racing out to tend to us. We halted them right away because we didn't want them to run over something we may have missed.

Immediately people swarmed the area. They stabilized Rogers and loaded him into the back of a Humvee to be medevac'd to Dogwood. They then rallied us in as we were relieved by other troops. That is when I first saw the hole, the hole that the explosion came out of that was intended to take many of our lives. I took my camera out and took a picture, as if my mental picture of it would fade one day.[65]

Those involved were then loaded into the back of the deuce that Blue drove and when all the drama happened, he broke the accelerator. We made it back to the prison though.

I helped to unload two SAWs of injured and started to walk in. I was first greeted by Maze bawling. She grabbed me and gave me an "I am so glad you are alive" hug. I continued towards the arms room to turn the weapons in where I was then embraced by Andy, along with his kisses all over my face. I was so happy to see my good friend.

I turned in all the weapons and walked to my

---

65. Reading this 20 years later, I still get emotional. Tears fill my eyes and there is a tightening in my throat. How we didn't lose anyone that day is beyond me. Rogers definitely got the worst of it, recovered in country, and stayed for the remainder of our mission. He was honored with a Purple Heart post deployment, as were many others.

area to drop all of my gear. That is about the time I broke down with my fellow soldiers and friends.[66]

Shortly thereafter, we received intel that the mine was remote detonated. There was spliced commo wire running from where the explosion went off to a small building by the schoolyard about 100 meters away. They brought the interpreter to that area to try and get some intel. We didn't find out too much that we didn't already know. I guess that we will just have to keep driving on. I am not sure what they are going to do to prevent this from happening again, but I hope they do something, and fast.

---

66. I bawled my eyes out. I was beyond frightened. I'm glad I allowed myself the release.

June 28, 2003

Last night was the hardest night I have had sleeping since we have been here. I was on QRF so I got to sleep most of the night, but I kept having messed up dreams. And I would wake up every 45 minutes to an hour hyperventilating. It was a very uncomfortable feeling.[67]

One of the first times that I woke up, I walked outside and happened to see Andy standing there. He just got back from the doctor. Turned out that he had been bitten by a camel spider and had three eggs in his toe. The surgeon cut it open and took the eggs out and let all the puss drain out.[68]

---

67. Basically I was reliving the day before over and over. Each time remembering a specific aspect of the event in extreme detail.

68. Yes, the spider laid eggs inside my friends toe. He wasn't the only one, another guy did too, but in his back. Lucky for Andy, they cut it out when they did. Apparently, if he had waited much longer, the babies would have hatched and eaten their way out. We have a spider that is a cousin to the camel spider in Las Vegas called a sun spider. I came home from a work trip sometime between 2007 and 2010 to one on my front door. I dropped my bags and considered burning my house down. I thought somehow a camel

So because our platoon is so short of people now, they divided us up into second and third and we are back to 12 hour days. Plus we opened up two more towers. I guess the company has requested that infantry come in and provide us with 360 security and put up some checkpoints on the freeway right next to us. I hope that happens. I might be able to sleep better at night.

I wrote mom this morning when I got off work. I told her a little of what happened and told her that I was okay. I didn't want her to see the incident on the news and wonder. I wanted her to be sure. I miss her so much. I wish that I could just be hugged by her and have her tell me everything is going to be all right. Hopefully I will get to talk to her soon. The commander has a satellite phone that he has been letting people call home on. Maybe I will be able to do so.

---

spider had followed me home and hid out all the years post deployment.

June 29, 2003

Last night I received my first letter from Dana. I was so happy to get it. But when I started to read, I got really sad. Three friends from high school, Chris Oxboro, Beau West, and Beau's girlfriend got into a car accident and none of them made it. I guess tragedy isn't only happening in Iraq. I kind of wish that she would have waited till I got back to the States to tell me, but she doesn't know what's happening here.[69]

I was a little overwhelmed with emotion at that point. It has been a really shocking last 48 hours. I spoke with the chaplain about all the emotions I was feeling. He spoke wise words, and I felt much better after talking with him.

Then shortly after, I was allowed to use the sat-

---

69. Note to anyone writing letters to those at combat. Fill the letter with positivity. Fill it will good memories. Fill it with the highlight reel you post on social media. There's enough negativity we are dealing with, and we very much look forward to letters, allowing our minds to go elsewhere, if even for a short moment in time.

ellite phone that the company has to call home. I called the house first, but I got the answering machine. So I then called the restaurant. Mom answered. It was so good to hear her voice. I told her about everything that had happened. She was mostly concerned for my safety and well-being. We talked for a good 20 minutes. I was so happy after speaking to her. She truly is my guardian angel.

June 30, 2003

The last day of June. Well, I am glad. This month has been nothing but horrible drama. I'm ready for a brand new month. Maybe July holds something better for me. I already know of one good thing that will happen, plus I'm getting my rank back.

I received a letter from Aunt Michelle and Uncle John tonight. Andy and Evan brought it out to my tower for me along with some goodies and my pill. They're such sweeties. Men like that are hard to come by these days. Most men are so self-indulged. I hate it so much.

Tonight was such a long night. 12 hours in a tower is just way too much. I fell asleep at least three or four times. One of the times, SFC Moore walked up on the tower to give us coffee and cookies. Thank goodness he didn't think I was asleep. I would have been in big trouble.

I was going to wake Andy up ██████████████

████████████████████████████ But
I decided that I am way too tired, so I won't bother
him. It is amazing what 12 hours of boredom can
do to you.

July 4, 2003

Well happy Independence Day America. I sure wish that I could have been home for the nation's birthday. Instead, I am stuck in the shit hole of all shit holes. It sucks too because it's Friday night, Fourth of July and I should be in Vegas getting drunk and watching fireworks. But nooooo!

On the second I finally got a day off. It was really nice not having to do a damn thing.

Then they started playing some Latin music and Evan got me up to dance. It was a lot of fun. He taught me a new dance and then we salsa'd. I almost felt like I wasn't here.

Then after a bit of that, they put on some house

and trance music. One of the signal guys, which happens to be from Vegas and is active duty in Germany, started to dance with the glow sticks. It was such a trip. I felt the vibe of Vegas.

When we finally left and walked out of our hidden away secret, it was like stepping out of one world right into another. Talk about a hit of reality. I was glad I had that night off though. I actually didn't mind working the next day. Actually, I was so refreshed that after I got off work, I took a shower and stayed up with Andy for a bit and then laid in my bed and stared at my mom's picture until I fell asleep.

Today I am working QRF. So it will be a pretty relaxed night as long as they don't make me relieve someone halfway through, like they have every other time.

I am supposed to get my rank back today. We'll see if anyone remembers. I think that I am going to be upset if they forget.

Well, it's about time to get ready for work.

I was sure glad to be on QRF tonight otherwise I would have missed the firework show. First sergeant and the commander let a couple troops shoot off five 203 rounds. They flew up and busted apart into a beautiful display of stars.[70] Plus, I am

---

70. To see a firework-like display on the Fourth of July, in a combat zone,

sure if I was home I would probably have eaten the same thing I did tonight. Barbecued hamburgers and hotdogs. It was good and it helped that I was really hungry.[71]

For being in Iraq, I really can't complain. God bless America.

---

by weapons ready to kill the enemy is like nothing I've ever experienced. Every Fourth, I think about this display and in turn think about the people I was there with. Loyalty took on an entirely different meaning after this deployment—meaning that I have rarely found outside of the military or law enforcement environment.

71. I honestly don't remember eating hamburgers and hotdogs. Now I'm curious as to where they got them and what they actually were.

July 6, 2003

Last night I worked on tower three with Carmen. I had not worked with him yet, so it was nice to hear some new stories.

Around 11 o'clock there was a really loud boom about 1500 meters north of us and then about 5 to 10 seconds after that there was another big boom. Only this one was in the sky and it was an explosion. Carmen said that it was anti-aircraft. Nothing else happened after that but you could tell everyone was startled.

I guess the rest of the company left and the living area had to go into the bomb shelter. They said they were there for about an hour, and they were sweating their balls off. In that way, I'm glad I was in a tower.

I haven't received any mail from my mom in a while now. It's been over a week. I really hope I hear from her soon. Hopefully I will be able to call her soon. We are now allowed one phone call per week, and it has now been about that. I miss that woman so much.

The days seem to be going by fast. Probably because all we do is work, sleep, work, sleep. Hopefully the days will keep on flying.

July 7, 2003

Well it seems as if we are starting to have a tradition here. Last night around the same as the night before, 22:00, there was another boom. Only this time it was an RPG, and it was a hell of a lot closer than any others have been. It was shot around the north entrance and was either shot at the sign out there that reads "Americans are friends of all Iraqi people"[72] or they missed and that is where it hit.

We had our QRF out there at the time, and they saw two people, one of which was carrying a tube like structure. They fired upon them, missed, and took them into custody. They were interrogated right away. Neither of their stories matched whatsoever. So they are being held in our prison.

This morning, QRF went out to go look and

---

72. I would absolutely LOVE to meet the person who thought it was a great idea to paint this on a billboard. Please find me, message me, I'll buy you a beer.

see if they could locate the RPG and anything else. They found the tail end of it. I took a picture.[73]

I had a dream last night that I received a big box from my mom. I woke up and there was no box. I was a little disappointed. I haven't gotten any mail still and I want to know what's going on.

Also, yesterday Red Cross came out to evaluate the living conditions of us and the prisoners. I am thinking that did not go so well. Because our whole mission has been nixed. They aren't going to work on the prison anymore and I guess they want the prison camp moved or something too. So for us, this could mean two things. One, we could be relocated and carry out the mission, or two, we could get ready to get redeployed back home. I really hope that it is the second one. Things only seem to be getting worse and a lot closer.[74]

---

73. I still have this picture as well as one showing the partial hole in the brick-like billboard they shot it in to.

74. I know it was probably just wishful thinking, but I don't know why I ever thought that just because a mission was disrupted, we would be sent home. After all of the hell we had to get through to get there, the chances of going home vs getting assigned another mission were slim to none. Also, if it gives you any formal indication of the unsanitary and unsafe conditions we were in, this is it. Still, we remained. I guess the mission was the priority.

July 8, 2003

It is starting to become a tradition for shit to get shot at us and blow things up at 22:00 now. Last night was the third night in a row. This time it was a little worse. First an RPG went off around the north gate and hit a building just in front of tower two. Then about 30 minutes later one went off by the west wall and hit the sign again. I guess they really hate that sign. But I say leave it there and keep painting it. I would rather the sign be the target than one of us.

It doesn't appear that they are trying to harm us because they aren't hitting us or damaging anything we have of value. Either that or they have really bad aim, and they are just practicing for the real thing. Meanwhile, scaring the shit out of us and getting everyone's panties in a bundle.

Our commander addressed us today at guard mount. He verified that the prison did in fact get nixed. What exactly this means for us, he wasn't sure.

Perrie and I came to the conclusion that they will discontinue sending any more prisoners here and then when the remaining of them get released and there isn't anyone left, we will go home.

I hope that I am right for once in my life. I still have a feeling I will probably be in Iraq for my birthday. And that really sucks.

So I am up on tower six tonight with Sgt Lauren. He is good company. This tower is quite close to the south wall and just on the other side of the wall is the highway. Filled with lots of Iraqi vehicles. Yeah, I don't feel too safe. If anything comes flying towards my head, I am going to jump out of the tower on the inside of the compound. Better two broken legs than a blown off head.[75]

I am really hungry. I hope they bring us our dinner soon.[76]

---

75. Such odd logic to have, but logic nonetheless.

76. How easily I go from talking about my head being blown off to thinking about food.

July 9, 2003

Last night at five minutes until 22:00, they hit again. Only this time it wasn't any RPGs or mortar rounds. They actually grew enough balls and came in with AK-47s. Our QRF couldn't pinpoint on where the fire was coming from, but it was definitely being fired towards us. QRF went out and swept the area and couldn't find the enemy. That is because they are cowards and never show their faces. They just fire and run, never looking back. It doesn't help that they have no common sense whatsoever. Last night was number four at the same time.

Tonight I sit in a Humvee by the prison yard for extra support if needed. I am glad that I am here instead of QRF where the rest of my platoon is. I don't want to be the one going outside of our wall looking for the enemy blind.

Sometimes I wonder if our leadership really

thinks about the life taking risks that they make us take.[77]

So it is around 21:30 now, which means in about half an hour we are going to be expecting another trying attack. Maybe tonight will be our night and they'll be caught off guard. I hope that is what happens. Then maybe they will stop playing these little games with us and we will be able to let our watches turn to 22:00 and not have to worry.

I received two letters from Kaylie today. One was pretty old and one fairly new. Yet they were postmarked recently. Mom probably forgot to mail them out. Still no mail from mom yet. My letters must be lost in one of those 42 Conexes [Container Express: cargo container] with mail somewhere.

I still haven't been able to call home yet either. Tomorrow I am going to try my ass off. I don't care if I have to make up some story.

Oh, also, I got a letter from mama last night. It was the first one I have received from her. It was really nice to hear from her. It made me think of my papa. And one of those long silences that you

---

77. Listen, I totally understand that part of our job as soldiers in the U.S. Army is to find and eliminate the enemy. However, given the circumstances (our company size, unarmored humvees, old weapons, and lack of protective equipment) I still don't feel the best decision was to send us out blindly looking. No reconnaissance. No satellite intelligence. No intel at all, quite frankly. Just the knowledge we had of their activity from the previous nights. I think the Iraqis were trying to understand our weaknesses and gauge our numbers while also trying to dial in their (really old) equipment.

always seem to have on the tower, my mind drifted away somewhere else. Somewhere back in time when I was a little girl. I could see his face and all I wanted at that very moment was for it to be real. To be able to embrace him and tell him how much I love him. I hope that he is proud of what I am doing here.[78]

I feel that there are only a few people that truly understand what I am going through and that is because they have already lived this moment in their lives. And now I understand the look in their eyes—the one they would give when someone asked them about the wars. I now understand why they did not say much and stood there in a trance. The only way you'll ever, ever truly know is to have experienced it. But then I would never wish for anyone to be here. I would rather them be clueless for the rest of their lives, and only know what the textbooks teach.

---

78. Papa, my grandfather, was the only real father figure in my life. He was a combat veteran himself—made it through three wars - and unfortunately, he lost his battle to cancer when I was just 13. It wrecked me. I think this is about the time I slipped down the slope of becoming that "lost 17-year-old" that felt she had no other option than to join the Army. I imagine if he was alive when I considered joining the military, he would have put a stop to it. Either way, I just know in my heart he is proud. Proud of my bravery, my perseverance, and my resourcefulness. We used to watch MacGyver together, a lot. I never heard any of his war stories. I never got to share this unspeakable bond we now share. The same bond I have with so many, some I may have yet to meet. Maybe you.

July 10, 2003

22:00 came last night and nothing happened except some gunfire. It wasn't close at all. Although the night was still filled with surprises. Around 23:00 one of the prisoners picked up a tent pole and started to charge at another prisoner with it. 400th's Rover saw it, cocked a shotgun, but by that time he had already swung and hit him across his head.

The whistles were blown, which means for everyone to get down. Indeed they did and while all of this is going on I am trying to load my rifle. It ended up double feeding, which is almost impossible to fix without assistance. So I left my 16 in the truck and cocked my 9. Everything settled down, we got the injured and the offender out of the cell. The injured had to be medevac'd, and the offender got handcuffed.

Then as I was writing mom at around 24:00, a big ass boom went off. I believe nobody knows what it was. I think that it was too far away. Which is fine with me. It did scare the crap out of me though. I thought my heart was going to jump out of my chest.

The rest of my shift was blurry. I kept drifting into the halfway point between sleep and awake. I was mostly on the sleep side.

Starting today, most of our platoon is back together. They brought in 10 soldiers from the 770th MP unit and put them with second platoon and moved the remaining of first and second squad back to night shift. That means Andy is back working with me, but it also means so is Sgt Beige. You win some, you lose some.

So now I am sitting in a hallway in the prison where the hadji's are working. I am supposed to keep an eye on them and make sure they are doing their job. I will only be here for about another hour, until they leave. Then I am off for the night until around 21:00, whenever it gets dark and have to go to the shower point. I have been pretty lucky getting these half shamming[79] shifts. They can keep this up all they want.

---

79 .The meaning of "shamming" is commonly used in the military to refer to people who are half-assing a task or to a task that is perceived to be easy. The official definition is anything that is not what it appears to be.

July 13, 2003

The 11th was a Thursday and there were no direct attacks made. I sat at shower point that night. I spoke with the medic, Geyzer from the 400th, that evening and he taught me a lot about the Iraqi religious ways that I didn't know. I feel that the information was needed. He said Thursdays are the Iraqi's holiday, like our Sundays. That is when they clean themselves of all their sin like actions. From sun up Thursday to sun up Friday, they pray. That is why most of their hostile acts are done on Fridays. Hence the riots and the deuce getting hit by the mine. So I was thinking, tonight will be okay. Everything should be pretty calm. But then I thought about Friday.

The 12th was a Friday and I was in tower six with Wess that evening. Around midnight I heard a thump. I looked around and didn't see anything. About 30 seconds later, there were two more thumps and another 15 seconds later there were three more. That is when the radio traffic got heavy.

Three mortar rounds landed in front of tower four, where Andy was, and one landed in front of tower three. It landed no less than 150 meters out but no more than 250 meters. So they were rather close, but not close enough to hit any of us.

Then a little bit later, after everything died down, tower four reported seeing a man walking our perimeter. He kept walking south, then tower five saw him, and then myself at tower six saw him. He wasn't doing anything at the time, but he could have been their spotter. So I figured we would go and swoop him up. There's plenty of probable cause. One, he was in violation of curfew, two, he was in an area that the mortar rounds could have been launched and three, for suspicious behavior. But did we go and get him, no, no, no. I think everyone forgot that we are the police out here. Luckily nothing else happened that night.[80]

The 12th I was on external QRF. I was a little scared because I knew I would have to go outside our walls.

The first mission we did, we released 19 prisoners. We loaded them all up in the back of the deuce

---

80 . Definitely getting desensitized at this point. There is something to be said about my thinking that six mortars being fired at us is lucky.

which Blue and I were driving and took them up the street to the highway and let them go. We made it there and back with no problems.

On the way back in I took a picture of the RPG sticking out of the sign that used to read "Americans are friends of all Iraqi people."

Then we relaxed for a little bit, ate, and then set out to set up some trip flares. We set two up at the north gate, and on our way over to the southwest corner to set up some more, we found three Iraqis inside the wall. They ran and jumped out the hole in the wall, just big enough for me to fit through and took off on their bikes. I am sure they were up to something. So we set up our trip flares and made our way back to base.

Then they sent four guys out to these foxholes about 250 to 300 meters south of the north gate. We were doing two, 3 1/2 hour shifts. I was on the second. Meanwhile, the rest of us just kicked it by tower two in our Humvees inside our wall.

Around 22:30 someone reported that they saw a light by our old west entrance. So, knowing it was going to happen, LT called us and told us he wanted us to go and check it out. We sat out there until 02:30 watching absolutely nothing. Plus, LT got this great idea in case mortar rounds started going off, Sergeant Beige and Blue would sneak around, climb into a tower on the exterior and observe where, what, and who, and maybe even engage. That never happened so that was good.

So at 02:30, instead of 00:30, we relieved the foxholes. Nothing happened the rest of the night and we came in at 03:45. Although, I think that they had attacked us enough earlier that day.

First I got woken up at 07:30, three hours after I had gotten off work. There were five prisoners that escaped. By the time I had got up and dressed, they caught them. Tower three had three of them at gunpoint, and the other two were over by the ECP. They still thought that count may have been off, so we were sent into the prison, to sweep it and clear it. We didn't find anybody. So we were then released to go back to bed.

Just as I was falling asleep, there was a thunderous boom that rattled my heart. It sounded just like the boom when they blew up the deuce. I jumped up, threw on my clothes, and ran outside to see what was going on and if I could help in any way. I was told that the 770th MPs left, and just outside the Northgate an RPG was fired at them and barely missed. But because the explosion was so close, the Humvee was still shaken up. There were no serious injuries, just a few minor cuts and bruises. I was very happy to hear that. I was really scared for my fellow soldiers.

Today I sit on tower five with Sgt Beige. I overlook the southeast corner of the exterior wall in the freeway that runs parallel with the south wall. I really don't know what to expect out of tonight. I really hope that nothing happens. I am really tired of having minor heart attacks.

I received a postcard from Mom last night. It was so great to hear from her. She said that my package shouldn't be too far behind, and I should be expecting it really soon. I'm looking forward to that package.

I received a card from mama today. It was cute. It said, "I have written you many times in my mind…Guess I should have used paper!" It was nice to hear from her again and so soon.

We got our DSN phones in yesterday. Only a few people got through. It's hard to get a connection and the line is always busy. I hope that when I try, they work. I would really enjoy talking to my mom. I haven't talked to her in about three weeks. I can't believe it has been that long.

July 15, 2003

The evening of the 13th the mortar attacks came in at 21:45. There were about four to six launches and I only remember hearing three explosions. It sounded really close. Probably because they were coming from the southeast corner and flying right over our heads. After that it stopped and nothing else happened the rest of the night.

Last night was a different story. I was on internal QRF with the rest of my squad, except Blue, who was on external QRF. I was sitting at Glenn's table, looking at a truck magazine and happened to see the most beautiful truck ever. It looked like an F250, but it was an Escalade. So anyway, I was admiring this truck and I heard a really large, wall-shaking boom. Everyone jumped up and started running for their equipment. I ran straight over to the QRF stage point, found Andy, and we waited there. Boom after boom came. Everyone from the QRF were pulled to go on the roof, except Andy and me. They told us to stay by the TOC [Tactical Operation Center] with Sgt Otto. Which was fine with me.

Things calmed down for about five to 10 minutes. Then the booms came again and again and sounded really close. One sounded as if it had hit the west wall by tower eight. It scared the shit out of me. I thought for sure that the next one was coming straight down in the middle of our living area.[81] They finally stopped though. Thank God! I thought that they were never going to stop, and we were going to get hit. Luckily no one was hurt or hit. It's a good thing that I was on QRF too because after that stressful night I went to sleep.[82]

This morning I woke up around 10:00. Andy and I decided that we were going to start doing PT. We went up to the rooftop and ran for 10 minutes and then came down and did as many push-ups and sit-ups as we could do.[83] Then I went back in-

---

81. Tears fill my eyes and I get goosebumps remembering the feeling of helplessness I felt that evening. To sit there, gauging the direction of where the mortars were coming from, the likely calculations they made to their fire during the silence, and the redirects in the next silent moment knowing they over or under shot but never knowing if they'd get it right this time. It was the most anxious feeling I've ever known. Just waiting for death, literally knocking, or more so booming, at the door.

82. How I fell asleep after that evening of events, I don't know. Honestly, I was probably exhausted from the adrenaline and anxiety and my brain just quit on me.

83. Working out is still my positive outlet when I feel triggered. I don't always remember this but when I do, I recover more quickly.

side and took a two-hour nap before having to get ready for work. Andy got lucky; he is off today.

So here I sit on tower five once again. Only tonight I have Carmen's company. I feel safe with him. He has prior active duty with an airborne infantry unit. So I think he has just a little bit of experience to guide me tonight when all hell breaks loose.

Tomorrow is my platoon's phone day. Whether they will work or not is a different story. But you bet I will be trying until I get through. No matter how long it takes. I need to hear my mom's voice badly. I miss her so much.

July 17, 2003

The evening of the 15th it was silent the entire night. Not one thing happened. It figures...we bring in two Bradleys and two snipers from 3rd ID and nothing goes down. It's all right though, because we were prepared for it, and that is what counts.[84]

That morning, when I got off shift, after I put all of my gear up, I went to stand in line to use the phone to call home. The phones weren't connecting well, and people were having a hard time getting through. Then I looked down and a very evil thought came across my mind.[85] The commander's cell phone was sitting on the table with a fully charged battery. And no one but Wess was around. I looked back up at Wess, and he looked at me. I could read his eyes. He said, "Take it and

---

84. Two months of hostile activity and we finally got support.

85. I think "evil" is a stretch, Dallas.

let's go." So I did. I unplugged the phone, stuck it in my pocket and started walking quickly outside. Wess followed shortly behind. We got up to the roof and I called my mom, I got the answering machine. I was so pissed. There was no way I just stole the commander's personal cell phone and was not going to be able to talk to anyone. So I passed the phone to Wess, told him to try. Just as I did, Lieutenant Bobby walked up.

"What are you doing?"

"Smoking."

"Oh."

She kept walking. I can't believe we pulled that off. I thought for sure we were caught. When she went back down Wess got on the phone and got through to his mom. I was glad for him. He hadn't spoken to her since we left Ft. Lewis. I tried again after he got off, got the answering machine, and gave up. We went back down and placed the phone right back where it was. I'm so sly sometimes.[86]

It wasn't enough, I needed to talk to my mom. So I sat down at the DSN phone. After about 20 times of dialing and hanging up, I got through. Hearing my mom say my name was all I needed.

---

86. I was so incredibly disappointed. To take such a risk with zero reward. I do remember feeling gratification in Wess' ability to chat with his people though. I'm curious to know what my commander would have said or done if we were caught.

I was so happy. We had a great conversation. Then mom handed the phone over to my sister. About five minutes into the conversation the phone cut out on me. I was really upset.

I tried and tried calling back, but all I got was a busy signal. Stupid operator. So I went to sleep and woke up at 11:00 to try to call again. There was a really long line, so I decided to bug the signal personnel and get them to let me use their line. I got through after about 10 tries. I talked to my sister first for a while and then I spoke to mom again. It was nice to be able to get out everything you want to say without being rushed. I was in such a great mood after.

Also, that evening Rambo got a Red Cross message saying that her mom was in the hospital with a brain hemorrhage. So the commander was going to let her go home. That afternoon she left. I was sad to see one of my best friends leave. But I know it was for the best. She took my film to get it developed for me. I thought that was really nice of her. Then I will be able to send pictures of this awful place home.[87]

---

87. This was such an emotional mind fuck for me. Here is one of my best friends freaking out because her mother is in the hospital, getting ready to be sent home to be with her and I felt jealous. I felt envious and mad and selfishly didn't want her to leave. Not that I didn't want her to be with her mom but more so that I needed her to be there with me. Rambo is one of those people that I just can't live through the ups and downs without. She is

Yesterday was my day off. It was nice not to have to do anything whatsoever. ███████

███████████████████████████████████████
███████████████████████████████████████
███████████████████████████████████ Three cars stopped on the overpass and shot two RPG's at us, missed, and by the time the third was going to fire, we had already opened fire on him. So he took off and the rest of the night was quiet.

Today I spent most of my before work time working. We have to clean up everything because we are expecting the secretary of defense's assistant. And Lord knows we can't let him see how we really live.[88]

Also, the last three days, Andy and I have started to work out. I am glad that I am getting myself back in shape. All I needed was a little motivation. I believe I'll continue the rest of the time we are here.

Tonight I sit in tower one with Sgt Beige. Yay! This will be another long 12 hours. Oh well, I'll get by. Hopefully. At least I am in a tower where currently nothing has come close to hitting anywhere around it.

---

still very much that person for me, even 20 years later.

88. This is often referred to as the "dog and pony show." It's always annoying and never convenient.

July 18, 2003

Last night around 23:00 the Iraqis struck again. Only this time we were fully ready for them. It only took about five minutes for one of the three Bradleys to change positions. They got up to the north entrance, and all hell broke out. I believe two RPGs were fired towards them, and that's all it took. The Bradleys lit them up from there. I was in tower one, so I saw the whole thing. It put such a great feeling in my heart to finally see us fight back.[89]

I guess this morning they were supposed to go out and recover any body parts. I'm not sure what they found. This morning, the secretary of defense's assistant came. Everyone was so paranoid and was putting on a show for him. I got up and had to go to the bathroom. I started to walk outside, and

---

89. This night is what I see, feel, smell, and hear every single Fourth of July. This was what I imagine the true feeling of being liberated felt like when our Independence Day was marked. The feeling is still raw and lives on the surface, something that I can tap in to at nearly any moment. A feeling and moment I'll treasure forever.

Lieutenant Bobby started yelling at me. She was telling me that I had to put on my uniform and full battle rattle. I told her all I had to do is piss, so she let me get away with just my flack vest and Kevlar. Then, when he came walking through, it seemed as if we had a red carpet laying out or something. There were like 20 secret service personnel following him around with AKs and M4s. I felt like I had done something wrong, and they were raiding the place. I also felt like a zoo animal. They were all just staring at us. I was glad to see him leave.[90]

Tonight I am working with internal QRF. So I should be able to sham most of the night, as long as they don't find something for me to do. Which will probably be the case.

---

90. All in an effort to make our command staff look good. Why not show them how we truly live? Maybe we would have received more support by ways of supplies, water, troops …

July 19, 2003

Tonight I am on tower seven, the only tower that I have not been on until now. Tower seven kind of sucks, too. First we have to watch the prisoners and second we have to watch 75% of the exterior. Also, all you smell is hadji shit all night long.

I am here on shift with Sgt Forder. He is one NCO that I actually have respect for. He is very laid-back but at the same time takes care of his troops.

Last night, internal QRF was very slow. Nothing happened on the outside, which is good, and nothing happened on the inside, which is even better. We did have to go out to the compound a couple of times but just for stuff like prisoners changing cells and headcount. Nothing big.

I fell asleep for about an hour outside while waiting for our shift to be over. When I woke up, my eye felt funny. It was swollen and irritated. So this morning, when I got up, after Andy and

I worked out, I went and saw the medic. He put some kind of dye to see if there were any scratches. There weren't. He said that if there would have been, I could have been medevac'd out of here. Life, limb, or eyeball.

So after that, he flushed my eye out and then put some kind of ointment in it that made everything blurry. He said that was normal and it would go away. It turned out to be a bug bite on the edge of my eyelashes. Stupid bugs.

Well it is 21:45 already and absolutely nothing has happened. I definitely think that we scared the shit out of them the other night. I say good. I sleep better at night knowing they are scared.

I received a letter from Kaylie's father last night. I think that it was really nice of him to write and check up on me. It took his letter almost 2 months to find me. Must have been lost behind some big package in a Conex somewhere.

Today I received a letter from my brother Nick. My eyes filled up with tears as I read it. It was great hearing from him. Now I want to see him. I have not seen any of my brothers in over a year now. I really wish I had a relationship with them.

I get to call home again in approximately 30 hours. It is going to be so nice being able to talk to mom and Kaylie on a regular basis and actually know when you are going to be able to call.

July 21, 2003

So far so good. Nothing has happened since the tanks lit the Iraqis a new asshole. I do believe that we scared the shit out of them. It's nice to have a quiet peaceful night and not have to worry about getting blown up.

Yesterday was a good day. Andy and I, along with the rest of the squad, took the snipers back to their camp. It was about 30 minutes away and when we got there, all we saw was blue. Their whole camp was circled around the lake. The first thing that popped into my head, and I know Andy's as well, was can we go swimming.

After some hard persuasion, we actually talked Sgt Beige into letting us go for 10 minutes. I was so scared that he would change his mind that I ran down to the shore, ripping my clothes off on the way. I got down there and dove right in. It was great. The water was perfect. After about 10 minutes of swimming around and a picture, Andy and

I crawled out of the lake, put our clothes back on, and headed back to reality.

Today I woke up and called home. I spoke to mom and Kaylie. I got through pretty fast, and I talked for a good 30 minutes. It was great to hear their voices again. Then Andy and I went outside to burn shit. It was my squad's detail today.

Then I came in and cleaned and rearranged my area. I have more room now and more privacy.

Tonight I'm on tower six with Sgt Forder. I believe we are going to watch some movies when it gets dark.

Dinner was good tonight. It was like McDonald's. It was egg and ham biscuits with hashbrowns. I hope that the cooks go back to cooking good stuff like tonight. Lately we have been having a lot of egg block.[91]

I got a letter from Dana yesterday. It was really nice to hear from her. It was a good letter.

---

91. How do I best describe egg block so that you may truly understand. Well, it's like you took a bunch of whisked eggs, poured them in a 9x13 pan, and then microwaved them. They all had the same texture but different tastes. Most days I would drown it in Tabasco sauce or just not eat. I couldn't get past the texture.

July 23, 2003

Well, I believe that I lost my purple pen and that makes me very upset. So I guess it will be black and pink now.

Tonight we got hit by mortar rounds again. It had been a week. I guess they had given us a long enough break. They were firing them about 800 to 900 meters south of my position and they were landing about 150 meters in front of me, just outside of the exterior wall. This time, I actually saw the explosion. It was like a big firework that went off on the ground. It would have been almost pretty if the intention wasn't to kill us.

The Bradleys went out to hunt them down and

found nothing, so we will probably get fired upon again tomorrow. I hate to say it, but it's likely. All we can do is say our prayers and hope for the best.

July 25, 2003

Last night I was on internal QRF. It was a pretty relaxed night. There were no mortar attacks, thank God.

Last night we started out processing all of our prisoners. They all left this morning. They are either being released or being transferred to another compound. We are making room for all of the Fedayeen that will be held here.

A lot of things will be different. These are people that have been brainwashed to hate us and trained to kill us. And not only will they do everything in their power to escape, but the ones on the outside will do anything to get them out. This is a huge operation going on in Iraq and it is crazy to think that the 72nd MP company from Las Vegas, Nevada National Guard is running the show. I never thought that I would be part of something this big, nor this important. My children and grandchildren will definitely be hearing some crazy stories.

Last night, as well as this morning I tried an hour each time calling home. I just couldn't get through. I guess I'll just have to keep trying.

August 2, 2003

Look, I found my purple pen![92]

It is already halfway through the second day of August. I can't believe that we have been here this long, nor how fast time is flying.

So the mortar attacks have died down a lot. We haven't had one in four days now. And the day we did, it was only one mortar that landed somewhere on the exterior perimeter.

Although three nights ago, we had a guy drive by on the highway that shot at TRP five. They returned fire and a few miles down the road the vehicle caught on fire. I am not sure what happened after that.

On 27 July we started receiving Fedayeen prisoners. Three of them. I helped pull security while they in-processed them. When they first come in

---

92. I would write with a purple and pink pen, alternating with the days or entries. Eventually these pens ran out of ink and my journal was filled with boring blue and black ink.

they are given a pat down search by the MPs that escorted them. Then they are screened by the MI. That is when they will decide if they are going to be worth interrogating or not, or if they are of any importance.

Next they are brought into the medic station. This is where they get their full body search. They're basically stripped down naked, their clothes are taken from them, and they have to bend over, spread their ass cheeks, and are anally probed.

It is great to see the discomfort on their faces. I asked the doctor if I could do the next one. He said he would let me, but he would get in trouble. They would be greatly offended if a female were to do the inspection. I just think about what some of these guys may have done to the females that were captured, and I want to make them feel a part of what the girls did.

Anyway, after the full body search, we dress them in a blue jumpsuit and then they are taken over to records. They are photographed, fingerprinted, a picture of their retina is taken, and they are tagged. Once all of that is finished, they are assigned to a cell and locked up. And from that moment, their lives as they know it are finished.

Since then, the three prisoners have multiplied into 90. And that was as of last night. Today I have seen two sets of Chinooks flying in, so we probably have more. Our prison has become quite the popular place. We have people here all the time.

Plus, not to mention the 320th MP battalion that now lives to the west of us in a compound similar to ours. In the big open field to the south of them, they built a compound big enough for 4,000 prisoners. They started getting prisoners four or five days ago. I am not sure how many they have right now, but I am sure it will be growing into the thousands before long.

The 400th MP battalion left yesterday. They got assigned another mission at one of the jails in downtown Baghdad. The thing that sucks about it is that not only will they be working there, but they will be living there as well. They really didn't want to go; they were just getting comfortable. Everything was established and we all had a routine down. I am sad about them leaving because I lost some friends that I had made. I did exchange addresses and phone numbers so that when we all get home from this nightmare, we will be able to get a hold of each other.

Now the 320th is running the inside of the cage. They do things a little different. For example, they are carrying 9 mm and shotguns inside the wire. They say that it is for their safety, but what is going to happen when one of the prisoners catches a guard off hand and snatches their weapon right from under them. Shit is going to hit the fan.

Last night while I was on shift, SFC Moore came over and gave me some very positive information. He said that it is a law that a National Guard unit is not to be deployed for more than two years without a six month break. So thanks to the Monterey deployment, the unit was on for 13 months, we need to be out of here around 2 October. So that will put us back home around the beginning of November. Yeah, just in time for the fall.

Some other information that I received and found very useful was that I can buy a vehicle through AAFES. I guess that when you are overseas, you can purchase a vehicle through AAFES. You just let them know what vehicle you want, and they put it in the computer system and when you get back to the States you go see AAFES again and you let them know where you're going to pick up the vehicle and they give you a VIP card. When you go to the dealership, you give them the card and you get the vehicle tax free and at manufacturer's price.

That was some of the best news I have heard since we have been in country. If I can get a car, I am going to get a Toyota Celica, yellow. I really want a truck, but I am not sure if I could afford it. My insurance is what is going to kill me. Oh well, I am just happy that I am going to save some money. Maybe this deployment will pay off in the end.

Also, SFC Moore mentioned to McGill that they may be starting an R and R session. Supposedly, they will fly us to this other small country south of here, put us in some kind of motel room, and I'm clueless to whatever is after that. As long as I had a real bed, shower, and a phone, I would be happy. But personally, I just don't see this happening. So I am just going to pretend that I never heard any such thing.

We were briefed today that our mail is going to be really messed up again. Since the 400th left, they took us off their APO so I am guessing we will be having a different one. Things were really starting to come together with the mail and now it is going to be all jacked up again.

Tonight I am in tower four. Right now I am by myself until McGill comes on at 20:00. Our leaders decided that only one person needs to be in the tower until dusk. So every once in a while, you will only have to work an eight hour shift. I was that lucky two days ago. This will be my second night in a row with McGill. He is good company though. Before last night, he and I haven't worked together in a while. Although, we may be running out of stories to tell each other.[93]

---

93. I recall a shift we spent together that illustrates just how close we all can get. McGill had a horrible upset stomach but there are no sick days in a war zone. So he paced around the tower endlessly. That was until he had somewhat resolved that situation and came to face another. He was going to shit. Now. And it wasn't going to be pleasant, or quiet. There are no bathrooms in the towers. There are no bathroom breaks. So what did we do? Great question. The men pissed off the side of the tower. Easy. I cut the top off a liter water bottle and would squat in the stairwell, peeing in it, and then pouring it off the side of the tower. Not as easy but it worked. Now the "number two" task, not so easy. Mostly we tried really hard to take care of that business outside of our 12 hours confined to a tower. Or...we did whatever was necessary. McGill emptied his MRE bag, gave me a look full of embarrassment and remorse, and then walked to the opposite side of the tower to relieve himself, loudly. We never spoke of it.

August 4, 2003

Tower six is my post, Sergeant Carmen is my partner, and these are the days of Iraq. As I look out over the compound of Camp Vigilant, I can't help but think back to when this place first became our home. No prisoners, just 100+ Nevada National Guard men and women living in a shit hole. Now we have a battalion sized element living here with the capability of holding 1,000 Fedayeen and 4,000 lawbreaking Iraqi citizens (Alibabas). Soon enough we will be up to those amounts.

Yesterday I took full advantage of working on QRF. I was asleep by 22:30, woke up at 23:30 to help take coffee to the towers, and right after I fell back asleep until shift change. I got a good 12 hours of sleep. I feel refreshed. Although not as refreshed as Barnes and Perrie are going to be when they return from Qatar.

They got to go on a four-day, three-night all expenses paid vacation. The battalion had two open slots for an R&R trip and they happened to be the lucky ones. I am happy for them, but I am a little upset that I am not getting my day off. I was scheduled for today but now I won't be off for another four days. The price you pay for another soldier's freedom.

Last night was quiet, although tonight they blew off about nine mortars. It was different this time, it seemed as if they weren't firing them at us. All of the splashes were in the village area. I thought that was pretty odd. Why would they be firing on their own people? I really couldn't say. This country is all messed up. Anything goes here.

It's going to take a good while and a whole lot of effort to get this place back up and running again. So other than that, it has been a pretty quiet night. Not too much gunfire going off tonight.

A general came by today. I am not sure which one or how many stars they had. Along with the general came about 30 reporters. They were interviewing all sorts of people. That was my queue to run and hide. So Andy and I went up to the rooftop to tan. I thought it would have been funny if they came up and started taking pictures. I could see the headlines now. "What soldiers do on their off time," with a picture of Andy and me laying on our PT mats trying to cover up our half naked bodies.

Boy would family and friends back home get a kick out of that. Luckily nothing like that happened and I got a few shades darker as well.

August 7, 2003

Right now I am sitting in an air-conditioned room that belongs to the 55th Med out-processing station, waiting for someone in my unit to come and pick me up. Yesterday morning, not too long after I got off work and went to sleep, I woke up with the worst gut pain that I have ever felt in my life. I rocked myself to sleep a few times, but I couldn't bear the pain. I was yelling for help, but no one was around to hear me. The pain was getting worse, and I knew I needed some help. Then I saw Meyers walk by and I yelled for her. She came quickly, and I told her what was going on, and she ran to get help. In a matter of seconds I was swarmed by people. Jayes, Bruck, Perry, Sly, and then Geyzer, our medic and my friend, came to me and took my hand.

Right there the chaos seemed to stop, and everyone was zoned out. All I heard was Bryan, and I was able to tell him what was wrong. The next thing I knew, I was being lifted off my cot onto a stretcher. The next voice I heard was Andy's. He sounded so scared for me. I was almost to the medic tent when I started to feel nauseous, and I began to dry heave. After I stopped that they sat me down in the tent, and the doc started to examine me.

Everywhere he touched I felt pain. Then I got the IV and I knew what was next, the shot that was supposed to stop nausea. Yeah, it made you feel cracked out. I asked them not to give it to me, but I guess they had to because in my arm it went. After that, things got a little blurry. I remember Geyzer talking to me and telling me what could be wrong, and I remember Sgt Mount, SFC Moore, and Jayes coming and talking to me. I remember Andy never leaving, except when he went and packed a bag for me. Then I started wondering why would Andy pack a bag before I realized I was going to be medevac'd.

I told whoever was listening that I didn't want to go on the helicopter. I guess they thought I needed that too because the next thing I remember, I was loaded on a Humvee and driven to the LZ [landing zone]. Perez was holding my hand the whole time. Cane, Salt, Mount, and Sly were all there too. Then I heard the chopper. They covered my face so I wouldn't get sandblasted, and then I was loaded off the Humvee and on to the chopper. Sgt Mount stayed with me, and I remember seeing this soldier, he was on the medevac. I felt comfortable with him. The ride was actually smooth from what I remember. I think I fell asleep.

When I awoke, I was being offloaded and loaded onto a four-wheeler looking vehicle. They took me to a tent, and I was then checked in.[94] A doctor, Major Gonzalez, came and examined me. Then I was taken to a dark x-ray room. This was the first time I had to stand up, and I almost fell over. The pain felt like 1,000 needles. I got on the table with the help of the medics. They took lots of x-rays of me. Then I was brought to a little room and was told to take off my shorts and underwear. So I did and laid on the table. The doc came back and gave me a full pelvic exam. I hated it. I felt so uncomfortable. I didn't like the way the doctor was looking at me, I wanted to yell at him to stop, but I couldn't. I knew that this exam needed to be done, whether the guy was a perv or not.[95]

Next I got an ultrasound and then a video camera was inserted into my 'tata' and they looked at all of my insides. It was then that I was told I had cysts

---

94. My memory of being offloaded and taken to the tent feels like a scene out of E.T. Remember when they turn the house into tent city and the guys are all walking around in their white suits? Yep, that scene!

95. I'll never truly know if it was the drugs, pain, and my imagination or if I was completely taken advantage of. I just know that every single red flag and siren was going off and I felt like there was absolutely nothing I could do about it. I felt violated and super uncomfortable.

on my ovary, my left one. I got a little scared then, but only in my head. I was completely out of it. All I wanted to do was sleep.

They left me in that room alone for a while, not sure exactly how long. I was so tired but every time I went to La La Land that stupid cracked out shot that I didn't want, would kick in. Fall asleep, wake up cracked out, fall asleep, wake up cracked out. It was that way for a while.

Then I was moved back to the first room. I was given a shot for the pain, a little bit later a pill — a blue one — then a little later a white one. And that's not to mention the seven IV bags I received. And after that last one, I was done, just like that. I wasn't given any information on what was wrong with me, just handed a bunch of paperwork, pills, and sent on my way.[96]

I was still out of it, but I found Sgt Mount, which was amazing considering how many drugs I was on. When I found him, we went to this tent full of cots with air conditioning. There I slept. I slept well. I was awakened by a deep, loud voice — a sergeant. He was giving instructions. Realizing I

---

96. I don't remember what the paperwork said. I've look for it in my files and military records, nothing. I have no idea what they gave me. Honestly that evening felt like a bad dream — fuzzy and blurry memories that seemed surreal. When I was sent on my way, I felt like I was in a tented maze. I didn't know where I was or where to go. I was completely unsupervised. Luckily I found my team leader.

couldn't take in all of this info right now, I looked over at Sgt Mount and saw that he was listening and went back to sleep.

Sgt Mount woke me for dinner, we ate, and when we came back, we were instructed to get on a deuce that would take us to Camp Anderson, where we would wait until morning to get a ride back up to BIAP [Baghdad International Airport].

When we got to Camp Anderson, we were given a convoy briefing for the following day, and then were brought to this little building where we would sleep for the night. Before we went to sleep that night, Sgt Mount and I went to the camp's movie theater and watched *Shanghai Nights*. It was really funny. I needed that.

I went to sleep and woke up at 05:15 and was out at formation at 06:20. We were briefed once more and then we all loaded up. It was about a 15 car convoy. It took about an hour and a half. We were brought to the 55th out process at BIAP and have been here since. Waiting and waiting.[97]

I really hope that our unit comes to get us soon. It's nice sitting in the air-conditioned room but I

---

97. I didn't have any of my weapons, so I laid down in the middle of the back of the deuce. I laid there praying. Praying for no attack. Other than my team leader's 9mm that he loaned me, I didn't have any way to defend us or myself. Not to mention, no protective gear. I felt helpless. Note to future people that may be involved in some sort of scenario like this…send your medivac-ee with their weapons.

want to go 'home'. I'm really tired and I want to see Andy. I want him to know that I'm all right.

So that has been my last two days. But before this, the night before that morning,

August 8, 2003

Yesterday when I finally got picked up and came back to camp, it was a great feeling. I was happy to be back, and the company was happy to see me. I spoke to the doctor, Major Keen, and we came to the conclusion that one of the cysts on my ovaries burst and the acidy fluid that is in the cyst is what was causing the pain. So until my body absorbs all the fluid, I'll be in pain.[98]

Doc gave me Tylenol-3 last night and boy did that knock me out and I was pain-free. Although I woke up at 01:00 after being asleep for two hours because of nightmares. I kept having dreams of surgeons surrounding me with staples in their hands.

I got up and talked to Andy for a bit and then Rambo for a bit longer and then went back to sleep.

Oh yeah, Rambo is back. I guess she was back the day I left. I was happy to see her.

---

98. Unfortunately, I've struggled with these issues most of my adult life.

Also when I came back to my area, I had a letter from my sister, a box from Aunt Michelle, a set of beautiful little shot glasses with a vase jug,[99] and a note from Lund along with the picture I wanted.

All the glasses and jugs were from the "war criminals."[100] I really care about many of the people here. Andy especially was so happy to see me. He gave me a huge hug. He had guessed what was wrong with me. He knew like my mom would know. It's crazy how well you can get to know a person when you want to. Thank God for friendships.

---

99. Still have these. They're not necessarily shot glasses so much as small cups to sip from. They're beautiful and I believe made from clay.

100. The "war criminals" were self-proclaimed based on their repetitive displeasing behavior. They like to march to the beat of their own drum, often going against what the command said or wanted. They weren't actually criminals, nor did they commit actual crimes. Just a rebellious over exaggeration.

August 10, 2003

Today is my third day of not working, not including the two days I was at the hospital in Dogwood. It was much needed, not just because I was on pain medication, but also to just recuperate.

Today is also my last day of medication. I hope that the pain is completely gone. Otherwise it is going to be a very, very long 12 hours wherever I am.

Tomorrow I start working day shift. I am not very happy about them switching me. I like night shift. I'm going to sweat my butt off while working days. Plus, days is when all the convoys go out. So when I am on escort, I'll be going out quite a bit. I guess that I'm all right with that. I just hope that they put me back on nights soon. And supposedly that should be when Halls comes back.[101]

---

101. I didn't like going outside the walls of the prison. There were too many uncontrollable situations. I felt safer in the walls of the prison where there was a set regimen. A matter of fact, I prefer environments and situations

I was supposed to call mom yesterday, but it slipped my mind. I won't forget today. She might think that something is wrong.

today that have set regimens. Correlation in my subconscious? I'm thinking yes.

August 11, 2003

Today is the first day of working day shift. It's totally opposite of nights. It's harder to stay awake at the beginning and you get four hours of coolness and four hours of hot, hot, hot. I brought five bottles of water, that's 2 1/2 gallons. I hope that's enough. I better drink it all too, because I'm already a heat casualty and I don't feel like getting stuck anymore this deployment. My veins need a break.

Found out yesterday that our medics and the doc are leaving. The 400th is selfish, so they are making them move back over to their camp until they find a different mission for them. I will miss my friends, plus the only actual doctor around.

August 13, 2003

Since I have started days, my days have gone by a lot quicker. Yesterday I worked at tower six from 04:00 to 10:00, then I was relieved by Meyers. So from 10:00 to 16:00 I was on QRF. Nothing needed a quick reaction to, so I slept.

After work I went and worked out with Maze and the LT of MI. Boy did they kick my butt. I felt good afterwards though. I am sore today.

Before I went to sleep, I called mom and talked to her. She did find out from the doctor that everything they did for me out here was right. So that made me feel a little better.

Today I am working at TRP5 [Target Reference Point] with Glenn. TRP5 is directly Southeast from tower five. I'm not too sure why they have people out here during the day, it's kind of pointless. Hey, I'm just another number.[102]

---

102. There seems to be a huge void in transparent communication in the

Today we have more VIPs coming in. Some Congressmen are going to be stopping by around 13:00. Not sure who they are or why they are coming here. I am just glad that I am way out here, so I don't have to deal with the bullshit. I didn't realize how political the military was…

We just had about half a dozen children down playing in the canal about 100 meters from our tower. Three of the children started to throw rocks at us and another child had a sword. So I called QRF and they came rather quickly. When the children saw the Humvee flying towards them, they took off running. QRF came to the base of our tower, we told them what went on, and they then began to walk towards the children. They basically told them to get out of here and not to cause any more trouble. I do have to give them some credit for throwing rocks at armed US soldiers. But how quickly their braveness turned to cowardness when Glenn raised his SAW, and they saw QRF flying down here.

It is now 14:51, we have about one hour left of

---

military. On one hand, I understand. As a parent, we do things and have rules in place that are not explained to our children because they will simply not understand and typically it's in their best interest. At the same time, a simplistic understanding can sometimes contribute to a more willing compliance. The feeling of not knowing can put you in a constant defensive mindset, continually seeking control. This can lead to defiance or delayed cooperation.

shift, and there is still no sign of any VIP showing. A matter of fact, I can almost guarantee that they won't show, just for the simple fact that the commander told everyone to stand down. Oh well, it doesn't hurt me any. Except that he may show up tomorrow and then I might have to deal with the political bullshit.

I accomplished writing four letters today. One to Kaylie, grandma, Dana, and Eric.

August 15, 2003

Just about halfway through the month. The days will start slowing down now. The days are also supposed to get shorter by seven minutes a day, and the nights are supposed to get cooler. I definitely can't wait until that happens.

Yesterday was long, yet a very short day of work. I was on escort, and we only had one mission and it wasn't until 13:00. So I went back to sleep at 05:30 and didn't wake up until 09:00. Then I did a whole lot of nothing until 13:00 and we went to the fuel point to fill up the fuel pod. After that, we were done.

I skipped working out to let my muscles rejuvenate. I'll start back up today. I'm still sore but not too bad.

Today I am the roaming guard outside the yard.

This morning I was talking to Penne and David. Wow … do those boys have some stories to tell. Penne plans on having a huge party when we get back. I can't wait for that.

So my day has just begun. I wonder where it will take me?

So here I am sitting in the Humvee minding my own business when a transmission comes over the CINCGAR [military radio]. All I hear is the ECP telling their base that three 82nd vehicles are here. My heart dropped. No way could I be that lucky. And I wasn't. When I went over to where they were, I realized they were infantry. Too bad he[103] wasn't with them though. This party is staying here a week. I guess I knew my own luck better than I thought.

---

103. "He" is a dear friend of mine that I met at basic training and care very much about.

August 17, 2003

Yesterday I was on QRF all day. As soon as we got released from guard mount, I grabbed a cot and went right back to sleep. At least until I was awakened for a QRF drill at 09:30. I probably could have gone [slept] all day, I hadn't been able to sleep the night before.

So then I got off work, and did my usual routine…workout, eat, shower, go to bed. Yeah, well, the last one didn't go so well. I was just getting ready to hit the sack but had to go to the bathroom first. Halfway there I heard a noise that I haven't heard in a while and wasn't looking forward to ever hearing again. It was the boom. The one that makes your heart about burst out of your chest and your breathing speed up automatically. It's as if you have no choice in the matter. Then there was a second boom, that's when I turned around, ran back to my AO [area of operation], and grabbed my gear.[104]

I overheard someone saying that one hit inside our compound in the corner by tower seven and the other hit in the big compound and blew up the fence line. That would explain the rapid gunfire I heard following the second boom.

I still had to use the bathroom, and there was no holding it. So I went and was followed by Andy, who overheard me saying where I was going. When I was done, I was approached by SSG Goose and asked if I knew where the extra stretchers were. I said yes and was sent to retrieve them.

The next thing I knew I was in the yard where everything happened helping Smith, the medic, and the rest of the combat lifesavers. When the wounded were all brought up to the aid station, it was obvious that Doc was going to need some help. That's where Brown, Hide, Gris, Andy, Maze, Pote, and I came in. The seven of us treated and made ready for medivac around 10 to 15 people. We bandaged, cleaned up, gave IVs, put neck braces on, amongst many other things for hours of the night we were all supposed to be sleeping.[105] It was

---

104. As I read this back, I feel myself getting anxiety, heart rate speeding up, shortness of breath … honestly, I'd like to not read anymore at this point. This is the feeling that I avoided for 20 years.

105. I was not a combat medic. Meaning I had never had formal training

the most crazy experience to date. Thank God that none of our people were hurt. Although I can't say much for pants being shitted.

SGT Forder was the one in tower seven and at that moment, if just prior he hadn't craved coffee and went inside the tower to get some, I'm not so sure he would be in that great of condition right now. He said when it happened, all he heard was cling, cling, cling, the sound of shrapnel hitting the tower. Thank you, Lord for protecting my soldiers and me.

Well, I finally got to bed and was woken up after four hours of sleep for guard mount. Now I sit in tower four telling my story. I can't wait until 10:00 when someone comes to relieve me and I can go inside, lay on my cot, and catch up on some lost sleep. [106]

---

or practice on how to administer an IV. All soldiers receive basic medical training to assess situations and apply "bandaid" solutions until proper medical treatment can be received. This night was my first time ever putting a needle in someone's vein. One of my peers gave me brief and rapid instruction on the first guy and then I was on my own. I missed, several times. I honestly felt bad for my patient. By the third or fourth guy, I had it down. It was the most intense on the job training I've ever had.

106. This day and event are referenced as an achievement in one of my recommendations for award writeups, ultimately leading to one of my two ARCOM (Army Commendation) medals.

August 19, 2003

My workday is almost over. 15 more minutes.

Today I worked within the triangle of living point and shower point security and the ECP. The day actually went by quite fast by moving around. I'm glad they do that.

Yesterday, first sergeant approached me and asked me to write down the names of all the people who were out helping with the wounded. So I did. I think we might get some kind of recognition for it. That's cool. Finally, I am appreciated.

August 21, 2003

Another exciting event happened yesterday. Our escort crew went to BIAP on their normal every day PX, fuel, and mail run. Only this time when they were leaving, the lead vehicle, holding Watts, Miller, and an LT from another unit got hit by a remote detonated bomb. They are lucky Iraqis are stupid and blew it off a couple seconds too soon. Otherwise, they would all be in a lot worse condition than what they are and at least one would not be here with us to talk about it.

Miller was the worst off. He took a lot of shrapnel to his body. But they are saying that he will be fine and may even report back to duty. Watts was a little shaken up and has lost some of his hearing temporarily.[107]

Yet again, 72 MPs have survived. Nothing can bring us down…Actually, we are just really lucky,

---

107. I believe both of them received Purple Hearts for this event.

have a lot of people saying prayers for us, and God is looking after us.

The Humvee, however, is not so fortunate. It lost the front right quarter panel, both passenger tires are shot, and it has a whole lot of holes. Although it did show a lot of heart by getting the boys all the way back to camp.[108]

---

108. All I can think about after reading and transcribing this entry is at this point I have completely compartmentalized my emotions. It's almost comical to read, but the emotional, mature woman that I am now weeps as I see the transition of a 19-year-old girl shutting down while looking for the humor in just about anything. Reflecting on this day, nearly 20 years later, I remember being very frightened. These men were my family. These men were my brothers. To see them wounded, hurt, and scared nearly destroyed me. However, being in a combat zone, doesn't offer much room for emotion. There had been so many close calls with no major injuries up to this point. It's as if your mind starts to trick you into thinking you're untouchable. This day was a reality check.

August 27, 2003

Yesterday I received the package my mom sent. It was much anticipated. There was so much stuff. I really don't think that I need another package the rest of my time I am here. The best part was the pile of pictures. They were of all the animals and mom and Kaylie at the lake. Also Kaylie's prom pictures were in there. She looked so beautiful.

I have been so bored lately. I find myself spending a lot of time alone. I find that it's probably a good thing. I have been thinking a lot about my life and what I want out of it. I have decided that my main priority will be school. I'm already two years behind. I need to catch up or at least start. I need to be 20. I don't need to worry about men and relationships.

I think I finally figured out why God put me here [Iraq]. It's because I needed to be taken out of the life I was making for myself and be given another chance to start over. Plus I'm making a lot of money in the meantime.[109]

Tomorrow I am on escort. So far we have three missions. Hopefully that will be all. I hate leaving this place.[110]

So August is almost over. It sure did fly. Maybe September and October will fly as well. I still can't believe that I will be spending my 20th birthday here. It's only 12 days away. I'm here with some good friends though. So I'm sure it won't be too bad. Although I know it could be a lot better.

You know I didn't realize how many hoes we have in the company. Every female except four have hooked up with someone on deployment. I thought that I wasn't going to be able to live without sex, but I do have my standards. These people just don't care. It's sad. About a week ago, one of the girls had thought she was pregnant. And she's the youngest one here. I guess some people just have to learn the hard way. Oh well, not my life.[111]

---

109. Such insight I had on the foundation the military and my service would have on my life. All of my success today stands upon this chapter of my life.

110. There was so much uncertainty outside of the prison walls. AKs, RPGs, IEDs ... at least I could somewhat control my environment inside the compound. It's weird to think I had a sense of security in such a dreadful place.

111. It sounds as though I am judging my sisters, I'm not. I just couldn't understand the desire in such a dirty, gross place. You're dirty. The place is dirty. Everything is just dirty. I suppose it was a way to mentally go elsewhere, to temporarily escape.

August 29, 2003

It's 06:30 in the morning in tower eight. I look down below me and see the Fedayeen prisoners start to rise. The new guys are always the ones to rise first. They can't sleep because their head is pondering too much. How did they get here? How long will they be here? What will happen eventually in the end? Not even I know the answers to those questions.

Then there are the ones who sleep in until they can't bear the heat anymore. Those are the guys that have been here the longest and try to escape this place through dreams. Just as I and every other soldier in this country do every day.

About five minutes ago, I observed two Toyota Landfinders come into our compound and around 8 to 10, what looked like civilians, but clearly were some kind of special team in the military, got out. Half walked over to the in-processing tent, where a prisoner was waiting. I couldn't see inside, but they were in there for about five minutes. When they came out, he had a flak jacket on and was in shackles. They brought him to the vehicles they drove in on, blindfolded him, put him in, and then left. The prisoner must have been of some high importance. Some of the other prisoners that were awake watched and seemed disturbed when they drove away with him. Maybe he knows where Saddam is and next week he will be captured or something. Who knows. I'm not high enough on the food chain to know that kind of stuff.[112]

Yesterday sure did wear me out. I was on escort all day. Our first mission was at 05:30 and they didn't stop until 4 PM. I drove for about a total of nine hours. I have not driven that much in one day since my high school rodeo days. As soon as I was off, I read some of my book and then fell asleep. I slept right through chow until 8 PM. I finally woke up, took a shower, smoked a black with my boys, and then went back to bed.

I finally got ahold of mom too. It was great to hear her voice. I miss her so much. I didn't get to

---

112. Quite frankly, hindsight, I am very happy to not have known who was who or what their specific involvement was. It was much easier to see the prisoners as a number rather than a person with a back story, good or bad. Stories tended to lead decisions out of the logical side of your brain into the emotional side. Emotional decisions were not typically in our best interest in this environment. This pattern has carried over into my personal life 20 years later. It has been both helpful and destructive. I believe the key is a healthy balance.

talk to Kaylie because the second time I called after getting disconnected it was late. She was asleep and had school. I can't believe she's a sophomore now. I guess we are both growing up.

September 1, 2003

Today was a very long fulfilling day. I worked as an escort. Our first mission's SP [starting point] time was 06:30 and we were going to be escorting SSG Black, SGT Spector, and LT Ross around wherever they wanted to go. It was going to be an all-day project.

First we drove to BIAP and dropped off the laundry at the quartermaster. SGT Spector found out that they are going to be closing soon because their machines are breaking. So now we are going to have to find another way of washing laundry. I hope that they find something because I really don't have time and I hate doing it by hand.[113]

While they were doing all the processes to get laundry turned in, Brown and I went exploring in a burnt, trashed part of the airport. Inside, I found

---

113. I hate laundry to this day. However, the humility this reflection brings to the surface is noted.

one of those carts that the stewardess serves their drinks out of on the plane. I confiscated it because I thought it would make a great storage place. It has three shelves and a door, so dust won't just walk in. Plus, it says Iraqi Airways on it so I thought it would be cool.

After that adventure, we drove to Camp Victory to eat and use the phone. Phone was first for me. I finally got ahold of Kaylie. We had a good conversation. I hadn't talked to her in a while, and it was good to hear her voice. When I was done, I met up with Brown to go eat. Although we soon found out that we were too late. Then when everyone met back up, we went to the 777th AO. There SSG Black was negotiating with someone to buy a big screen TV for our MWR.

September 6, 2003

We had the biggest VIP come in today. Donald Rumsfeld made an appearance at Abu Ghraib, Camp Vigilant. SFC Lees told us yesterday at guard mount, and everyone was very amazed that the Secretary of Defense was coming here. We busted our asses yesterday cleaning this place up so that everything would look nice, and he didn't even come to our AO.

I used Rambo's video camera to tape the entire procedure. First two Apaches flew about scouting the area for about 30 minutes. Then, two Blackhawks landed, and I'm still confused on why they did. I think maybe the general flew in on it. After that, two Chinooks landed, followed by three Blackhawks. The last one had Mr. Rumsfeld on it. Press reporters were on the rest of them. When he got off the chopper, he walked towards the buses that we had for their transportation. But instead of going on the bus, he went inside the prison where the death chamber was. That's when I found Rambo and we followed him.

When we got inside, we were up close and personal. And just as he was leaving, he passed by me, looked my way, and shook my hand. He seems really nice. His escorts were trying to rush him in and out and he made a point to take his time, take pictures, and shake hands. He eventually left and will be back on his way to the States this evening.

Starting Monday morning, which happens to be my birthday, we are taking over the camp outside. So all of Camp Vigilant will be under our control. Which means things will finally run our way, but in return we have more people working, less people off, and longer periods of time without a day off. What sucks the worst is that they decided to do all of this on my birthday. Which I had scheduled off. Maybe SGT Combs will be generous and I'll still get it off. That is like the only thing that I wanted. I guess I'll just have to wait and see.

SFC Moore got intel today from the MI that we are supposed to get attacked with mortars again tonight. They are supposed to be the big ones and five to eight are supposed to drop. This scares me because two times ago, they were just over our AO. Last time they were just under and just maybe this time they will hit the target. One of these days their percentage is going to kick in and we are not going to be so lucky anymore.

September 8, 2003

Happy birthday to me, happy birthday to me, happy birthday dear me, happy birthday to me.

All right, I am not a teenager anymore. 20 years young and feeling great. For being in Iraq, my day actually went great. I have some pretty awesome friends here that put a lot of effort into making me happy and feeling like I was home.

When I woke up, Rambo and I cooked pancakes and ate them with peaches. They were really tasty! Then we went outside where Meyers and others had decorated an area with the things my grandma had sent to me. It looked like an eight-year-old birthday party set up. It was great. I loved it. They also got a big brownie cake from the MKT [Mobile Kitchen Trailer] and had my candles on it. They sang happy birthday to me, and then Andy and Barnes smashed my face into the cake. I had brownie all over my face.

After I went and cleaned up, I opened all of my

presents. I couldn't believe that they had bought me stuff. It was so cute too. They had wrapped it in newspaper. Rambo's even had a bow. I got two stuffed animals, one being a singing camel, and the other a teddy bear that wore an Operation Iraqi Freedom shirt. I also received a silver chain with cross, two bottles of perfume, an Operation Desert Scorpion shirt, a beautiful headscarf, a friendship egg, and a lot of cards. Those are mostly from my family.

In my Aunt Glenna's card, she said that when I return home, she is going to bring me to LA where we will then go to Catalina or go on a cruise for three days, my choice. That's so awesome. I have never done either of those things and I'm looking very forward to experiencing it. Especially with Aunt Glenna. She kicks ass. She's a lot of fun to hang out with.

Then the card from my Uncle Pat said that when I get home, he, Jason, Allan, and Shawn are going to take me out. I do believe that it will probably involve a lot of alcohol.

Everyone else sent their best regards and said I had presents waiting for me back there. I really love my family. They are great.

Rambo videotaped everything. I'm so excited to show mom when I get back. When we watched it, we were laughing really hard. There are a lot of comical events. Plus two EODs went off and shots were fired in the background. Mom will love that one. All in all, it was a great day, especially considering where I am.[114]

---

114. Not sure why I didn't write about it, but General Karpinski visited the prison this day. She walked through while we were celebrating. We all thought we were going to be yelled at or in trouble. Not the case at all. She stopped, inquired as to what we were celebrating, wished me happy birthday, and then showed me how to properly wear the hijab (scarf) I was given.

September 9, 2003

It is really chilly this morning. I think that it is probably around 80° and I am cold. That's a big drop in temperature though. It's at least a 40° difference.

Today I am working out in the yard. I really don't like being out here because the prisoners are perverted, and I feel really uncomfortable. Maybe it will be different with the Fedayeen prisoners. They should have just a tad bit more class. We'll see. [115]

---

115. I feel like I didn't elaborate because I was too disgusted to even write it down. That would have made the nightmare real. Sometimes I would shake off events as though I just woke from a terrible dream, quickly moving on to the next thing, anything. So, allow me to elaborate now because even still, these memories live on the surface—too easily recalled in detail. In fact, I struggle to write it now. I'm on the verge of tears. My stomach is churning, and I feel sick with anger. When I speak of the perverted behavior…here's what I mean: Every so often we were required to do a head count, ensuring none of the prisoners had escaped while also checking on their wellbeing. Sometimes we also went through their things looking for contraband (weapons, etc.). The EPW camp had several cells or areas and within those cells were a large tent or two filled with cots for the prisoners to sleep or rest on. I would cringe at the thought of walking through the tent for a couple of reasons. First, it was dangerous. I could have been overpowered

I have a feeling that it is going to be a long day though. Especially with Lenard and Glenn assigned to the same area as me. They drive me crazy. All they like to talk about is a bunch of political bullshit. Glenn thinks he has a logical explanation behind everything. I think that he is full of shit. It doesn't help that Lenard throws gasoline on his already burning fire. I wish that I could just go to sleep.

---

and taken as a hostage, leveraged for an escape. I could have been hurt or killed, out of spite. I took precaution, and relied on my training, but there is absolutely nothing that could have prepared me for the prisoners' behavior. Second, some of the prisoners would take note of my working the inside of the camp that day and make a point of being in the tent when it came time for head count. I would walk into the tent hearing and knowing before actually seeing. They were masturbating while looking me dead in the eyes, keeping their eyes on me the entire time. I had never felt so violated. I had never felt so disgusted and uncomfortable in my life. The worst part, there was nothing I could do. I had to endure this a few times before I found any and all reasons to work any place other than inside the EPW camp. Even still, when I would work the perimeter of the camp, some would come crouch at the fence, pull out their dicks to show me while fondling themselves. I would pretend like I didn't see them. I would pretend like it didn't bother me. I would pretend like I was feeling nothing at all. And apparently, I would pretend like it never even happened, seeing as I couldn't even write about it in my own journal. I can't help but think this is why I didn't write in the journal again for another 12 days.

September 21, 2003

Last night was the worst night that I have spent in Iraq. At 9:30 PM the Iraqis started another mortar attack on Abu Ghraib. This time we weren't so lucky. I hated to say it, but I knew it was coming. The odds would have to play in sometime.

There are three MI tents out by the yard and have been for about a month. In one of those tents there are soldiers that sleep and guard the valuable equipment. That tent was greeted last night by one mortar round, flying into the side of it. Nine soldiers were hit by its shrapnel. Only eight were medevac'd.

One brave soldier lost his life last night. I send my blessings to his family. Two of the guys that were medevac'd, I was friends with. One being Dugan from the signal unit, and the other being Johnson from the MI unit. They said Dugan should be all right. He took shrapnel to the back and head. He is lucky. Johnson took it to his arm and shoulder. The medic said he may lose his arm.

I feel that I am a pretty strong person that can hold my own when the going gets tough, and express myself later, but last night was different. It was just too much to see my friends in the position they were in. I finally lost it. I wouldn't even know how to express the way I was feeling at that time. It was stress, anger, sadness, guilt, and terror all at once. I didn't know what was coming or going. All I wanted to do is hug my mom and have her tell me that everything was going to be alright. I eventually cried myself to sleep.

When I woke up this morning, it reminded me of an event that happened just over two years ago — September 11. Not the actual event itself, but the way people acted afterwards. Everyone was very quiet with their heads very low.

Everyone is handling it their own way, but I know we are all feeling the same thing. Sorrow. And thankfulness. Thankful that we are still alive. That almost sounds wrong, but I know everyone feels that because I do.

It could have easily been me. Rambo and I had talked about that last night. There are stairs just outside of the yard tower where we have gone to just talk and get away from everyone. About 20 feet from that spot is where the mortar round hit. I'm thankful I wasn't out there last night.

I just wonder when this will all end. Not just

for us as a company, but for everyone in Iraq in the same position I am in. I am so tired of hearing about lost lives, when all we are here to do is help, and most of us would rather be home anyway.

In some ways, I don't blame them because they were brainwashed into Saddam's ways while growing up. But as humans we can all think for ourselves, have our own opinions, and do as we choose. You may keep it inside, but you don't have to act it out. Why do these people not think about what is being done?

In some ways, I blame the military officials and our president. They have us in here trying to rebuild and help Iraq before the war is even over. It just makes it that much harder. What is the real reason we are here? I don't think I will ever know that. But for the higher ups that do, I hope that it's worth it.[116]

---

116. It took me nearly two weeks to transcribe this entry from its written version to digital. I read the first line, shut the journal, and avoided it as I had done for 20 years. At this point I didn't know if I was going to be able to complete this project. I've been reminded of this event, or rather the people, occasionally on the anniversary through social media. Most often I would allow my internal eye to see their faces, blink, and then find anything more distracting. I know now that this was, simply put, avoidance. I knew I wouldn't be able to face this entry alone. I also knew that I did not have to. I am grateful to have people who surround me with love, acceptance, and can be brave when I am not.

September 23, 2003

Today I went to 28th CSH [Combat Support Hospital]. They are located at the palace with four heads just on the outskirts of Baghdad. It was really pretty there. Plus, it was like a little city that the army had built within a city.[117]

The reason I went there was to get my wisdom teeth looked at by the dentist. They have been causing me a lot of pain lately. I think they are trying to come in. Anyway, I went and the LTC said "Yeah, they need to come out, but I don't want to do it here considering the environment." I was like, "Alright I guess that I'll just suffer the rest of the deployment." So when I came back Lieutenant Bobby asked me what had happened, and I told her. She said that was unacceptable and she would see

---

117. The "four heads" were statues of Saddam Hussein towering three stories high. The palace was the Republican Palace, and the heads were removed in December 2003.

what she could do. I hope that she finds something, because this is ridiculous.

September 25, 2003

I went and saw the dentist today. He was a really nice guy. He's in the National Guard, so he is down to earth and civilized. He actually asked me what I wanted. So I told him ... I want the pain to go away. So he said that I would have to go get x-rays and then he would see what he could do.

After I went and got x-rays and came back, he looked at them and told me that it would probably be best if I got one side at a time taken out. I said all right, and he got down to business. I was really scared at first because they couldn't knock me out, they just had to numb me up a whole lot. I didn't think it was going to be enough. But it turned out it was. All I felt was pressure. Boy was I swollen when he was done! It was very hard for me to talk, and all I wanted to do was go to sleep. But that didn't happen.[118]

---

118. I'm very surprised that I didn't elaborate on the environment. It was

Instead, we went to the PX. We waited there for the rest of our convoy to come. While we were waiting, two vehicles rolled up that I had never seen before in my life. It turned out that they were Italian special forces, paratroopers, military police. And they were hot! The vehicles were crazy looking though. Their equipment was great. They looked like they were part of the LAPD swat team or something. I need to go to Italy. Beautiful land and beautiful men. [119]

Anyway, I finally got back, took my Percocet, and passed out. It's a good thing I have quarters tomorrow because I'm going to be up for a while from sleeping all day. Maybe I'll be able to eat something tomorrow as well.

---

like nothing I've experienced before. It was like a scene in a horror film. It was an ill-lit, small warehouse. A dental patient chair sat in the middle with a couple spotlights illuminating it. Around the chair were trays filled with the typical dental tools. I remember thinking to myself, "Am I going to be murdered today?" I think I was in too much pain to read into it too much. My teeth were growing in sideways towards the rest of my teeth. Ultimately compressing them together. My jaws ached in pain. Eating was mentally and physically a struggle. It had to stop. Recently, my oldest son had to have his wisdom teeth surgically removed at nearly the same age I was. I told him, his dentist, and the oral surgeon this story. They all looked at me similarly, in disbelief.

119. The military did end up taking me to Italy in 2005. It did not disappoint.

September 26, 2003

Today was a pretty relaxed day, although it was rather painful. I woke up feeling like shit, my mouth ached so bad. The first thing I did was pop a pill in my mouth. My cheek was twice as big as yesterday. After the pain started to go away, I finally got out of bed. I went and got some movies and then made myself at home in the MWR room. I had my blanket and pillow, and I was all sprawled out. Almost felt like I was at home. Yeah, right! I only wish.

After two movies and a nap, I made my way back to the area and slept some more. I did a lot of sleeping today. I think that I made up for all of the lost sleep over the last four months.[120]

---

120. Not. Even. Close.

September 27, 2003

I sat in tower six today for 12 lovely hours. Actually, I slept most of the time. I was on Percocet, so it wasn't like I could help it or anything. It was my chain of command's decision to put me back to work, even though I was still on a narcotic. Oh well, nothing happened, thank God.[121]

When I came in after work, I had a package waiting for me. It was from my Grandma and it said Halloween package number one. Considering the birthday packages I had received; I was very curious to see what was in this one. When I opened it, I found a clown wig, funny glasses, a happy Halloween sign, Halloween rubber bands that glow in the dark, and a bunch of Halloween candy. I got a bunch of people to put on the clown wig and I took

---

121 I understand that we were (always) short staffed but to put me in a tower, with a weapon, in charge of guarding and securing perimeters … well I don't believe anyone would say that was a good decision.

pictures. It was really funny. Thank you Grandma for making my holidays that much better!

September 28, 2003

Today went by really fast, especially for being in a really slow position for 12 hours. I was at sally port[122] and Penne was the roving shotgun, so he hung out with me all day. So did a lot of other people. It seems like everyone stopped by to chat for a little bit. We had the radio bumping and Penne even brought out his hookah. Good company makes the day go by faster.

Then after work, we had a squad meeting. When it was finished, Meyers had two bottles of shaving cream in her hands and gave me that look. Brown just happened to be right there. So I grabbed the other can and we covered him with shaving cream. Then I ran because I knew that my payback was coming. I hid well for a while, but he found me with Joe's help and got me back. I was covered from

---

122. A "sally port" is a guarded and controlled entry way to an enclosure. In this case, the EPW camp.

head to toe. The bad part was that I had just taken a shower. What comes around goes around.

October 1, 2003

Good Lord, I can't believe I have lived to see an-other month in Iraq. It is so hard to believe that it is October. September flew right on by. Hopefully we will be going home soon. Oh how I hate this place. I can't wait to go home!

October 2, 2003

I went and got my other two wisdom teeth out today. I wasn't as scared as last time because I knew what to expect. Although these teeth were a lot tougher to get out. I was really sore when he was finished. Luckily, this time I got to go straight back to base. Well, at least it is done and over with. Plus it was all free. Well, kind of. I wouldn't call coming all the way to Iraq, fighting for your country, and risking your life to get your wisdom teeth taken out, free exactly. At least I got two days of quarters this time. Now I'll get lots and lots of sleep. I definitely deserve it.

October 4, 2003

I have been on quarters yesterday and today. Boy have I slept a lot. I just hope that I can fall asleep tonight, so that I can work tomorrow at 03:00.

This afternoon SFC Moore pulled all of us in first platoon that are on dayshift to a meeting. He told us some excellent news. He said that everyone should be leaving this godforsaken place on the 20th of October. Headquarters and some others (volunteers) will be leaving the 16th to drive the vehicles back. The rest of us will be flying from BIAP. I am so excited. Finally we are leaving this place. I want to call my mom and tell her. She will be so relieved to hear this news. I just hope that the commander is putting out correct information. I would hate to see what this company would do to him if he got our hopes up once again. I'll be praying for us.

October 5, 2003

The yard kept me preoccupied today. Those prisoners sure did keep us busy. It all started with this one guy who kept staring at me. He wouldn't take his eyes off of me and I was really annoyed. So I took him out, placed him in handcuffs, and let him think about it for a while. After he sat on his knees in the dirt for a half an hour, I told him that it was very disrespectful, and to not let me catch him again. I didn't see his eyes for the rest of the day.

Then three guys decided that they wanted to get in a fight. After we pulled them out and placed them in handcuffs and listened to their stories, I could not help but laugh. One dude went and sat on two dude's bed and was trying to talk him into giving him some 'pokey-pokey.'"[123] One dude also

123. This term was often used by Iraqis to describe any type of sexual activity in English. I'm sure they learned it from an American. Or maybe TV. The majority of inappropriate, wrong, or weird things that the Iraqis said in English were taught by someone with the primary motivation to laugh at them. As I've said before, humor is most often used as a coping mechanism

has a bladder problem. So when two dude said no, and then saw poop slipping out of his poop bag, he said hell no. So one dude got all butt hurt and started to kick two dudes ass. Then three dude came in and saw two dude getting his ass beat. (Two dude was three dudes boyfriend) Then he started to jump in. So it was just one big lovers fight. They all just wanted some booty. Now, do you see some of the things I have to deal with?

Then throughout the day we had to apprehend another for trying to escape, another for throwing rocks, and two more for fighting. It was a busy day. I was sure glad when it was over.

---

while dealing with traumatic situations.

October 6, 2003

I worked in the prison today with the females. We now have five females in custody. One is 16 years old and accused of being a suicide bomber, one is 17 and arrested for trespassing, one is 22 arrested for prostitution (her husband is here as well), and the other two look like they are in their late 40s and were arrested for being BATTH party members. They all seem harmless though and they act nothing like the males. I can actually talk to them.

Today they drew my picture and read my future with cards. It's crazy though, because they know nothing about me, yet everything they told me made sense. Maybe it was just a coincidence, but I rather believe it.

October 7, 2003

I went and picked up the 1st Sgt and the crew that went with him to Kuwait today. They had gone down there to get more detail on the five W's of going home. It turns out that the commander made up the dates he gave us and didn't have any clue to as what he was talking about. Yes, we should be leaving around that time, but it is not official yet. They still have a couple more things that they have to take care of.

This is exactly what I was talking about. When I said, I hope the commander doesn't get our hopes up. For crying out loud, some people have begun to pack. That man is going to cause someone to have a stroke. I just hope that everything works out and we all leave around those times. I don't think I have it in me to call my mom and tell her otherwise. She will probably end up in the hospital. I hate being misinformed. I just wish that these people would get their story straight.

October 8, 2003

Well today has been an all-out shitty day. First, I am told that I am being moved back to night shift. I guess Sgt Daren and Petros have been bitching about a day off. And the only way they will get one is if there is another female (me). Therefore, I have to go back working a shift that I can't stand. I don't like the people, I don't like the hours, and it scares the shit out of me being outside of these walls at night.

Which brings me to the second reason my day was horrible. Four mortars hit tonight. Two just outside tower six and two just outside the wall of the warehouse that we live in. Rambo and I were in the arms room recording on her video camera when everything happened. The last two hit about 50 meters from where we were standing. Thank God for the thick walls. It was so loud, and I could have sworn that my heart stopped beating for half a second. That was just way too close for my liking. It was only about 75 meters from where I sleep every night. Which is where I usually would have been if I was not trying to stay up all night.

We have six days left until we hand our mission over to the other company and then everyone will be working days and they have to move me now. If I were SFC Moore, I would have told them to suck it up and drive on. We won't be here too much longer and won't be working any more in six days. I don't see what the big deal is. When we first got here, we didn't have a day off for about a month and a half. People have just gotten spoiled, that's all.

Oh well, I guess that I will just have to suck it up and drive on for the bitchers. It's a good thing that I have respect for SFC Moore, otherwise I would have spoken my mind. And believe me, most here have learned not to encourage that. What can I say? I'm strong minded. I learned from my mama. I love you mom. XOXO

October 12, 2003

Last three days I have woken up to a loud, obnoxious banging. Now, after five months of being in the sandbox of hell, our command has hired the Iraqis to install air conditioning units into the warehouse. We are scheduled to leave this place in one to two weeks and now we get air?! Would I be wrong if I said that I thought that was fucked up?! I did not think so either.

So now that I have been working night shift and already having a hard time sleeping, getting used to the time change, I also get to wake up to the sound of banging and the sight of Iraqi workers. I really didn't think that this place could get much worse. But it never fails to prove me wrong.

I had last night off, amazingly, and enjoyed the company of my good friends here while watching *Too Fast Too Furious*. Great movie! I wish Vin was in it though.

Tonight I am working at the hospital, once

again, babysitting an adult with a baby. This woman's baby is 12 days old and was born right here in Abu Ghraib prison. How sad. This woman is here for murder. The baby will be taken from her as soon as they find someone to care for it. Yes, it's sad that the baby will never really know his mother, but that is the price the mother will have to pay. I just hope this little boy doesn't grow up with bad thoughts of Americans and one day become our enemy. I can only pray for him.

October 17, 2003

[REDACTED]

Today we were told that the brigade commander has a copy of our orders. That is such great news. Now we can actually work on getting home. Plus, we have a little bit of a head start on our projected dates.

I packed most of my stuff today. I really hate packing, but I don't mind it when it has to deal with getting out of this hell hole. I didn't realize how much stuff I had accumulated in these past six months. Most of it I gave to "charity." I kept the food to get me by the next week or so that we are here. Then we will be down in Arifjan eating chow hall all the time.

The last two nights [REDACTED]

October 20, 2003

I woke up at 05:30 this morning and left at 06:00 on a journey to BIAP. This is the first time in months that my squad has moved as one unit. It feels strange to work with them again. My squad leader hadn't been out since my "swimming day." So there were new things that he was in awe about.

We went to Camp Victory, ate breakfast, used the phones, went to the PX, and then ate lunch at the 400th. I got back around 14:00 with no problems and nothing left to do for the rest of the day. Well at least, that is what I thought.

About five minutes after I had changed, we had to get back into uniform to go to formation to take the company photo. We also took a platoon photo and a squad photo. I have copies of all, and they turned out all right.

Later on in the day, I had remembered that tomorrow is Sgt Forder's birthday. And since he is one of the few NCOs that I respect, I really wanted to get him something. But I had nothing. So Andy and I found a card and wrote in it, and I told him I would buy him a drink in Fort Lewis. I'm sure he will be appreciative of it. So it has been a really long day. I'm glad it's over.

October 27, 2003

Yesterday our first sergeant and our commander left on a mission. Last night around 18:00, when it got dark, everyone was wondering where our two leaders were. The rumor is that they went to hunt down our orders. They have not yet returned, but it is still early in the day.

Other people are saying that they went on R & R. If that is the case, they are going to have a lot of pissed off soldiers. That just would not be right. But I really don't think that is what's up. I just hope they come back with our orders so that we can get the hell out of this place.

I find myself getting more depressed by the day. All I have time to do is think and it makes me sad. I think about mom and Kaylie, my friends back home, college I could be attending, and lately a lot

Today I feel really tired, so I think I'll sleep most of the day. Especially because tomorrow I have to work 20:00 to 04:00. That will be a tough night for me.

October 28, 2003

Around 18:00 last night we received a WARNO that we were going to get hit with mortars that were chemical. So that scared me a bit because I really hate even the mention of NBC. I went and got my mask out, made sure it was clean, and even tried it on to make sure I had a seal.

Everything was cool until around 21:00. I was sitting in my area visiting with my friend, Vixton, when SSG Beige came and told me to get in full battle rattle. So I got dressed as fast as I could and went to find some more information. I was told that there were two vehicles loaded up with machine guns driving close to our camp. And since 82nd wasn't out, we had to have everyone on standby and ready to go just in case something went down. So there I sat in full battle rattle for the next two hours when they told us to stand down. Nothing happened last night, thank God. But if it would have, we would have been ready for it. Better safe than sorry.

November 1, 2003

Another month started in Iraq. I can't believe it.

Yesterday was Halloween and we made the best of it. Rambo, Bitts, Maze, Penne, and I threw a Halloween party in the MWR room. We all dressed up, and so did many others. Rambo was a clown, Bitts was a cheetah, Maze was a Coke addict, Penne was a hadji prisoner, and I was a Barbie cat. We all looked really cute. I actually felt like a woman. Rambo broke out her make up and Meyers broke out her curling iron. We had a bunch of candy, soda, near beer, and music. A lot of people came, and it was a lot of fun. I almost felt like I wasn't in Iraq. I danced my ass off and was actually sore this morning. I was also sick.

My stomach has been upset all day. Nothing is worse than being sick here. Not only do you have a porta potty as your bathroom, but you have to walk 100 feet to get to it. So God help you when anything suddenly has to come out.

So we are supposed to leave this hell hole on the third. I don't think that is going to happen. I really don't know when we will leave this place. Nobody briefs us on anything. We are lost in the dark. I hate not being informed of anything. But what can I do. I am a slave in this world they call Army.

I haven't talked to Mom or Kaylie in a while. I just don't have the patience anymore to use our phones. I'm fed up with just about everything here. I'm very ready to return home and back to my real life.

November 2, 2003

The day started out with the arrival of Lieutenant General Sanchez, Iraq's commanding officer. I'm not sure what his visit was for. I caught a glimpse of him and walked the other way. That's just too many stars on one head for me.

Then I was informed of a very tragic event. A Chinook was flying from up north somewhere to BIAP. Some soldiers were going on leave to their homes, their families. Unfortunately, it was shot down by two missiles. The second Chinook following hovered before landing, putting the fire out and rescuing the survivors. 14 US soldiers were killed, and another 21 were injured. Just when they thought they were safe and on their way home, the worst happened. I feel for their families and pray for the injured.

I was told that we are now flying out the sixth. Again, I will believe it when I see it. I was informed this evening that our flight out of here is on the sixth now. But that too will get canceled if our orders do not arrive. All of our lives depend on this one piece of paper.

November 8, 2003

The evening of the 2nd everyone was notified that we had our hard orders. Everybody was so happy. This meant we could actually leave this place one day. On the 3rd one of our E-6s, SSG Randit went down to the airport and made flight reservations for those of us who are flying out. He came back with three possible dates, the 5th, 6th, and 7th. The transportation unit that is supposed to load our Conexes and broken vehicles on the convoy is supposed to show up any day.

The night of the 5th I was called to a squad meeting. SSG Beige put out that our plane was leaving the 7th and our SP time was 13:00. The convoy, unfortunately, was still waiting on the transportation unit and would stay at Abu until they arrived.

That night I hung out with Vixton from the 519 MI [Military Intelligence] Battalion. Over the last week, we had become really close friends. We understand each other on such a different level. He is a great guy and I enjoy his company.

The night of the 6th

Andy had Conex guard from 8 to 11.[124] So Vixton and I went out there around 8:30 to hang out with him. Everyone else showed up about a half hour later. We stayed there until Sgt Forder came to replace Andy. Then we went to Vixton's tent. And since I had to work at 1:30, everyone stayed up with me. Then I started out to the motor pool to do my shift. Around 02:30, Vixton came back from the internet cafe and kept me company until 04:00 when I got off.

I was awakened on the 7th at 07:00. Everyone was going crazy packing up last things and making a whole lot of noise. So I got up and got the remainder of my things together.

---

124. I find it very intriguing to see my mind flip into 12-hour time when up until this point I was writing in only 24-time. I discussed this with a friend that has a background in mental health. She shared that maybe subconsciously I was preparing to be home.

I went and visited with friends that I had made that I possibly will never see again,which made me really sad. That is why I chose not to say goodbye to Vixton. I only hope he understands.

So we loaded up all of our shit at 12:00 and rolled out by 13:00. We got to the airport around 14:00. There we had to palletize our bags to be ready to be put on the plane. Then we waited around for about three hours. I slept. The first plane was supposed to leave around 18:30 but that came and went. At around 19:45 they called for the second chalk, which I was on. So we went outside, had roll call, and loaded up on the C130 waiting for us. We left shortly after.

The takeoff is cool. Because we are in combat, they start the motors running really fast as if you're already flying. The whole plane was shaking. Then it takes off like a roller coaster. Then once it is in the air, it starts to incline by a 45° angle. It felt almost straight up and down.

Then we flew over Baghdad. The lights were everywhere, and it really did look beautiful. I do have to say that it was a great way to see Iraq for the very last time.

Soon after, I fell asleep and woke up when we landed. I couldn't believe that we were no longer in Iraq anymore. We now were in Kuwait and had just about nothing to worry about. When we got off the plane we got onto a bus which took us to a group of buses, where SSG Sammy was waiting for us. We then loaded our stuff on the two buses reserved for us. A bunch of us then walked to get some food. Subway was open and that sounded better than ever. I had a teriyaki chicken sub. Was the best 12 inches I've ever eaten. I scarfed it down so fast.

So we found out that the other plane hadn't flown out after us. So we left to Arifjan. When we got there, we brought all our stuff in and made ourselves at home once again. Rambo and I then went and took a long, hot shower. It felt so great. I scrubbed myself until I was raw. I felt so clean when I was done. I then came in and went to sleep in a real bed with a real mattress. I slept so great. Well that was until the rest of our crew came rolling in all loud and woke me up. Then we had formation. The first sergeant told us the do's and don'ts and gave us the heads up on what was going to go down. Basically nothing is going to be happening for a while. We have formation at 09:00 tomorrow so maybe we will find out more then.

After the formation, Rambo and I went to the PX to get laundry soap. On the way back we stopped at Baskin Robbins. I got a German chocolate and pralines and cream sundae. It was great. Then we went and did laundry. I washed everything. Even the supposedly clean stuff. Everything smells so good afterwards. I even washed my teddy bear. He smells clean now too.

When we were finished with that, we walked around until chow. The DFAC [Dining Facilities Administration Center] was really good. Either that or we have just been deprived for a really long time and don't know what good food is anymore.

Then I went and called mom. She was so happy to hear from me, and even happier to hear that we were now in Kuwait. She started to cry, and then I started to cry, and it was endless. I can't wait to go home and give her the biggest hug ever. I miss her so much.

After talking to her, I was so happy and motivated. I went to work out, then took a great shower. And then made my way back to the PX and bought a beautiful warm fuzzy leopard blanket. I love it. I also bought a blue one for my sister and also a diamond sapphire and pink stone ring. It's really pretty. Mom and Kaylie really made out this Christmas. I enjoy buying for them.

Well it has been a long, tiring day, and I think I'll retire for the evening. Good night.

November 10, 2003

Yesterday's excitement was going to the pool. I didn't have my bathing suit, so I went in my sports bra and shorts. I didn't get in the pool though. It was really cold. So I just tanned or at least tried to.

Then I went and talked to the AAAFES car sales guy about buying a vehicle. It sounded like a great deal. I called my mom that night to talk to her about it to see what she thought. She thought it was a great idea.

So today I went down there and bought a F150, 4x4 Ford. It's a 2004 and will be built just for me. I put $8,731 down and will be financed for $16,000. My payments will be for around $315. I am so excited. The only bad thing is that I won't have it until the end of February. But it is worth the wait.

So the convoy rolled in this afternoon. I was happy to see that they made it here safely. I didn't realize how bad Iraq made us stink until they came around when we were clean. They said that the day we left, that night, someone on the highway shot an RPG at tower five. Nobody was injured, thank God. I think that I will always think about that place and pray for the people that are and will be there. I know what they are going through and will always hope the best for them.

Tonight I pigged out. I ate the chow hall food, ice cream at the chow hall, then a piece of pizza and an ice cream cone from Baskin Robbins. I'll have to work my ass off working out tomorrow morning.

I called mom and told her about my truck. She was very happy for me.

November 13, 2003

On the 11th I had to get up with my squad at 23:00 Actually, I never really went to bed. We went to the wash rack to clean our four vehicles. Third squad had already been there for six hours, and only had one vehicle finished. Sgt Mount and I worked on one while the others worked on the other two. We scrubbed them until one in the morning[125] when they shut down the high-pressure hoses. So for about another hour and a half we did what we could. I was soaking wet, and it was cold outside. I am surprised that I didn't get sick. I think after being in Iraq for six months, I am immune to just about anything. So SFC Moore finally said that was enough and dismissed us. We cleaned up the mess we had made and headed back to the ware-house. I was so exhausted I just took off my wet

---

125. Again, with the flip on time format. Interesting.

clothes and climbed into bed. I didn't wake up until 11:30 the next morning.

I heard then that our vehicles had passed inspection, so I was really happy to hear that. Only one more major task to accomplish, and we would be ready for our flight home.

After I woke up, I ate pizza, did laundry, and went back to bed for just about the remainder of the day. Andy woke me up at 18:30. I went and took a shower and then we went to eat. This morning we had formation at 09:00. We turned in our vests with our plates. I was really hoping to keep those. They were the best and we will probably never see them again.

After the formation, I went to the post office and mailed all of my Christmas presents home. I have to call mom and make sure she doesn't open them when they arrive.

Then we had another formation at 13:00 in uniform. It was to prep us to go to class at 14:00. We had a Finance and JAG [Judge Advocate General's Corps] briefing. Then we were screened by the medical doctors. We had to tell them just about everything that went on in the deployment. They saved it all on this little card, it kind of looks like a credit card and I will give that to the doctors in Fort Lewis. I sure hope that I don't lose it.

Now I sit out by the Conexes pulling guard

once again. I hate these damn things and hope to never see one again. But I know I will. I'll only be out here for four hours, but even that can seem like a really long time.

Tomorrow morning we have to be up at 04:30 to be dressed and in formation at 05:00. We are coming out to the Conexes to have them cleaned and inspected. It's going to be a chore but well worth it. Because once that is done, we will have nothing left to do in this country and be ready to fly home. Well, at least to Fort Lewis.

They are saying that we have a flight reserved for the 19th. If that is the case, we may make it home for Thanksgiving. That would be a miracle. I refuse to believe it though until it is final. Better safe than sad.

November 23, 2003

We are still in Kuwait, but we finally got a flight. Our flight leaves on the 25th. So not too much longer. Although it feels like we will never leave.

The last 10 days have been nothing but relaxing, which has been really nice. We got our vehicles cleaned and our Conexes inspected. We also had a medical screening. Everything else will be done in Fort Lewis. We should only be in Fort Lewis for six or seven days, so that puts us back in Vegas in about 10 days. I still can't believe it. I can't wait to see mom and Kaylie. It has been so long, and I miss them so much.

Soon this will all be over and just a bad memory for me to tell my children and grandchildren.[126]

---

126. And apparently the entire world.

November 26, 2003

Well, I can't believe it, but we made it back to the States. We left Arifjan around 09:00 on the 25th and went to Camp Wolf. There we had customs go through all of our stuff. Then after we waited until 19:00 to board the plane. We had a 747 all to ourselves. There is so much room, half the plane was empty.

We stopped in Czech for a three hour layover. Everyone went straight to the bar. I bought our first round—Coronas. Then we had two Czech beers. They had a very different taste but were good. I was drunk. When we got back on the plane, I laid down in my chair and passed out. I woke up an hour outside of Washington [state].

When we landed, our battalion commander, Colonel, and some others were there to welcome us back to the States. When I walked off the plane, I started to cry. I couldn't help it, it came naturally. I don't think that I could have been happier.

We went inside where a band was playing for us, and then the General gave a speech. It was very moving. Then we made our way to the barracks in Fort Lewis. We unloaded all of our gear, settled in, and then made our way to the SRP [Soldier Readiness Processing] site. They checked our TB [tuberculosis test] and now we are just sitting around. My TB came back negative, thank God.

Oh, and the State [of Nevada] surprised us with a four-day pass to go home for Thanksgiving. I couldn't believe it. When I called my mom this morning, she was so happy. I can't wait to see her. Which is in like three hours. I am going to see my mom for the first time in 10 months in three hours. Oh, I can't wait.

AFTER THE JOURNAL

My mom, sister, and a couple of friends were waiting for me on the tarmac when we landed at Nellis Airforce Base in Las Vegas, Nevada. Even after 20 years, I can still feel the warmth of their embrace.

My mom made all my favorites for Thanksgiving dinner, and I slept off and on a lot, easily startled, and always unsure of where I was when I awoke.

Life immediately after my combat tour is fuzzy. I don't remember too much. Mostly memories of what my mom told me I did or was like. But there are three specific events that come to the surface:

I didn't leave my mother's side much in the first couple of months. We were on complete opposite sleeping schedules. When I could sleep—which you would think I'd have no problem doing after months of sleep deprivation—she seemed to always be at arm's length.

I went with her to get hay for the horses one

morning. She backed the truck up to the haystack and then got out of the truck. A few moments later I found myself on the floorboard of the truck in the fetal position.

The feed store help had dropped the first bale into the back of the truck from several feet above, causing a loud, thunderous boom and rattle. I'm not sure how long I was there. Only that my mother found me, peeling my arms from my legs, reminding me of where I was.

Towards the end of June, my mom and I were leaving the grocery store, walking through the parking lot and suddenly I found myself hiding under a stranger's vehicle with my mom on her hands and knees coaxing me out, again reminding me of where I was while simultaneously cursing the naive children prematurely lighting off fireworks. I still don't like fireworks. Especially premature ones. Or popping balloons.

Mid December I was startled awake by my mom excitedly yelling "They got 'em!" "They got him, Dallas!" She had learned of Saddam's capture and clearly wanted to share.

I sat, staring at the television, waiting for some sort of feeling that resembled closure. It never happened.

Around the time life started to feel normal again, the scandal at the Abu Gharib prison was publicized. I was extremely disappointed and very angry. My unit was immediately placed under investigation. We were challenged on our integrity and morality. Even though we were quickly found innocent of any illicit activity or involvement in the matter, it was heartbreaking to have these values questioned, considering all we had managed to live through. Not to mention that even 20 years later I feel inclined to explain the exact time frames of my deployment and find myself on the defensive when questioned as to my location or mission in Iraq.

After Iraq, I applied to work on one-year ADSW (Active Duty Special Work) orders with the Nevada National Guard Counter-drug Task Force. It was similar to an advanced D.A.R.E. program, educating 8th grade students about the negative effects of drugs. We also led summer camps for at risk adolescents currently in the juvenile justice system. It was one of the most rewarding years in my career.

I heard about an intel position opening up one day at work and was very intrigued to learn more. After doing so and being vetted by key management positions, I was offered one-year orders to work along-side DEA intelligence analysts in support of large narcotic investigations. My original goal after joining the military was now coming to life.

As the conflict in Afghanistan started to escalate again towards mid-2006 and now having a one-year-old son, I decided I would not reenlist. I shared and asked my DEA employed manager for a civilian position. Approximately six months later I was given that opportunity and continued to support the DEA in an appointed position with the Las Vegas Metropolitan Police Department for another eight years.

I was then recruited into corporate America to represent intelligence and investigative software I had used throughout my career. I am currently an executive in a technology company focused on addressing key challenges analysts face today. It is such a pleasure to come full circle to enable my peers with better tools to protect communities and organizations worldwide. I also volunteer my time, donning my analyst hat again, hunting human traffickers and identifying their victims while working with law enforcement all over the country.

I will forever be grateful for the solid foundation the Army laid at the base of my successful career. As well as the incredible people I'd rather refer to as my family. However, the traumas that I have kept locked away for two decades have brought many challenges in my personal life.

I now live in Montana and have two boys, 13 years apart, that share a birthday. They are my everything. My first gave me the motivation and drive to succeed, no matter my past experiences. He gave me a real purpose. My second inspires me to continue to chase my dreams, makes me laugh until I cry, and keeps me young at heart. I found my way back to horses and spend much of my 'me time' with them.

REFLECTION

In 2014, I attended a sales training preparing me for my new role in corporate America. I struggled to corelate my past experience with the business world. One of my evaluators and mentors, a Vietnam combat veteran, took the time to chat with me, learn about me. It was during these conversations he learned of my service in the military and law enforcement; and also of the journal I kept. He planted a seed deep in my subconscious, suggesting I publish the journal. At the time I laughed at this idea. Moreso because that would mean I would actually have to read it. (He is now the publisher of my book.)

Occasionally, I would pick up the journal, turn to the day's date however many years ago, and read an entry. Sometimes, they made me laugh. Others made me cry. Many times, they made me angry. I would close the book, internally vowing to not open it again. In 19 years, I had never read it in its entirety, until now.

It took me six months to read and transcribe the journal I kept 20 years ago in a foreign country. I knew this journey would lead me to open doors I had slammed and locked shut causing me to face emotions I didn't feel strong enough to ever endure. Therefore, I set a couple ground rules in place to protect myself.

One, this was a journey—my journey. Not a task assigned with a deadline. If I got through it, awesome. If not, no sweat. I didn't want the pressure of timelines.

Two, I would focus on the immediate goal at hand: read and transcribe the journal. The people I chose to share this endeavor with would ask me when it would be released, what the title was, or if I was going to self-publish. My answer was always the same. I did not know, and I needed to complete my first mission before I would even consider those other things.

I hit several road bumps during this journey. At times, I thought them to be concrete walls and my mission to be over. Two key things allowed me to continue: time and help. I could not have got through this process if it weren't for ground rule number one, my supporting friends, and my incredible holistic therapist, Heather McAbee. I will be forever grateful.

As I read, typed, and reread the words of a

19-year-old version of myself, the doors were unlocked, memories were unleashed, and deprived emotions flooded my mind. I knew in order to reach my goal I would need to submerge myself into the feelings. Whatever I might have felt during the process, I would not power through it. I would pause. Allow myself to see, hear, smell, taste and feel everything that was brought to the surface. This was the most difficult thing I had ever set out to do on purpose. But I soon realized, the quicker I submit myself to it, the better I would feel afterwards.

In the military, law enforcement, and even the corporate realm, vulnerability is looked at as a sign of weakness. "Rub some dirt on it." "Get over it." "Crying is for pussies." "Suck it up." "Don't be a Sally." These are just a handful of the sayings I heard over the years discouraging the acknowledgement, let alone an open forum discussion, of my feelings. Couple that with the immediate threat of revoking my security clearance if I had been diagnosed with PTSD following my deployment and you have all the reasons I never sought help. I chose to only discuss my experiences and feelings with those that were there with me or had been in very similar situations.

As I viewed my younger self from a 30,000 foot perspective, I saw the evolution of an emotionally unavailable young woman with wounds so deep, they may never fully heal. But I also saw strength, power, and sturdiness. Brene Brown says you cannot have courage without vulnerability. This book is a living testament to that statement. I share some of my deepest, darkest moments with you during one of the most trying times in my life in order to inspire you. To have a voice. To speak your truth. To embrace all life's lessons and use them as ammunition in your quest to leave one hell of a stamp on this world. Thank you for hearing my story.

I leave you with a quote that has grown roots into my soul, and I try hard to remember every single day:

> *You are the only you there is and ever will be. I repeat, you are the only you there is and ever will be. Do not deny the world its one and only chance to bask in your brilliance.*
>
> —Jen Sincero

ACKNOWLEDGEMENTS

To the Army, I thank you for the core values you instilled in me—values I still carry today and teach to my sons. Thank you for showing me what true loyalty is as it was demonstrated by my brothers and sisters in arms on countless occasions. Thank you for giving me a sense of duty, a reason, a purpose. Thank you for showing me how to properly earn respect. Thank you for giving me the opportunity to selflessly serve my country, my community, and my family. Thank you for allowing me to carry my head high, being proud of my accomplishments—all with honor.

Thank you for teaching me my most highly valued attribute of all: integrity. This word holds so much weight in my home. Thank you for the opportunity for me to choose personal courage because it truly is a choice. One that does not come without vulnerability and sacrifice. Lastly, thank you for being the foundation of my successful career and the platform of this book.

To Kristen, thank you for organizing a powerful and inspiring group of incredible women that encouraged me to find my strength and pursue all my dreams. To the 4Cs group, thank you for laughing, crying, yelling, and dancing with me. Your support and continued love will never be forgotten. To Heather, there are no words, but we don't need them, do we. You will forever be cherished.

To the Babcock's, thank you for implanting such a crazy idea in my head nine years ago and then helping me to bring that idea to life.

To my sons, Malachi and Rylan, thank you for breathing life into my soul and giving me the ultimate reason to choose strength and perseverance every single day. I love you.

Unlock the untold stories and dive deeper into *Shattered Reflections* with exclusive content featuring behind the scenes insight, in-depth discussion of the book's journal entries with Dallas's friends and family and hear from other combat veteran experiences.

Join us on Patreon for a unique journey beyond the pages. Discover more at Patreon.com/notsoAverageJane